# Junior Worldmark Encyclopedia of Foods and Recipes of the World

Junior
Worldmark
Encyclopedia of

# Foods and Recipes of the World

Karen L. Hanson, Editor

GALE GROUP

★

THOMSON LEARNING

*Detroit • New York • San Diego • San Francisco*
*Boston • New Haven, Conn. • Waterville, Maine*
*London • Munich*

VOLUME **1**

Algeria to France

# JUNIOR WORLDMARK ENCYCLOPEDIA OF FOODS AND RECIPES OF THE WORLD

Karen Hanson, *Editor*
Susan Bevan Gall, *Consulting Editor*
Timothy L. Gall, *Managing Editor*
Barbara Walker Dickinson, Janet Fenn, Rebecca Nelson Ferguson, Patricia Hale, Tara Hohne,
    Jennifer Jackson, Dianne K. Daeg de Mott, Rosalie Wieder, *Contributors*
Bram Lambrecht, *Graphics and Layout*
Jennifer Wallace, *Editorial Assistant*

## U•X•L Staff

Allison McNeill, *U•X•L Senior Editor*
Carol DeKane Nagel, *U•X•L Managing Editor*
Thomas L. Romig, *U•X•L Publisher*
Evi Seoud, *Assistant Manager, Composition Purchasing and Electronic Prepress*
Rita Wimberley, *Senior Buyer*
Michelle DiMercurio, *Cover Designer*

Front cover images © PhotoDisc 1995; back cover—Mother warming milk, India *(EPD Photos/Himanee Gupta);* Orange Salad, Brazil *(EPD Photos);* Saudi boy welcomes visitors, Saudi Arabia *(EPD Photos/Brown W. Cannon III).*

0-7876-5423-X (set)
0-7876-5424-8 (v1)
0-7876-5425-6 (v2)
0-7876-5426-4 (v3)
0-7876-5427-2 (v4)

**Library of Congress Cataloging-in-Publication Data**

Junior Worldmark encyclopedia of foods and recipes of the world / Karen Hanson, editor.
        p.  cm.
Includes bibliographical references and index.
Summary: Profiles the food, recipes, and culture of sixty countries.
        ISBN 0-7876-5423-X (set)
1. Food--Encyclopedias, Juvenile. 2. Cookery,
International--Encyclopedias, Juvenile. [1. Food--Encyclopedias. 2.
Cookery, International--Encyclopedias.]  I. Title:  Food and recipes of
the world. II. Hanson, Karen, 1977-
        TX349 .J86  2001
        641.3 ' 003 -- dc21
                                                                    2001035563

10 9 8 7 6 5 4 3 2 1

# Contents

READER'S GUIDE ...................................................... vii

MEASUREMENTS AND CONVERSIONS ............................. xi

GETTING STARTED WIH COOKING ............................... xii

GLOSSARY ..............................................................xv

ALGERIA ................................................................ 1

ARGENTINA .......................................................... 11

AUSTRALIA ........................................................... 19

AUSTRALIA: ABORIGINES AND BUSH TUCKER ......................... 29

BRAZIL ................................................................ 37

BRAZIL: AFRO-BRAZILIAN ........................................ 45

CAMEROON ........................................................... 53

CANADA .............................................................. 61

CANADA: FRENCH CANADIANS ................................. 69

CANADA: ABORIGINALS .......................................... 77

CHILE ................................................................. 83

CHINA ................................................................ 93

CÔTE D'IVOIRE .....................................................103

CUBA .................................................................113

CZECH REPUBLIC ..................................................123

EGYPT ................................................................131

ETHIOPIA ............................................................143

FRANCE ..............................................................151

# Reader's Guide

*Junior Worldmark Encyclopedia of Foods and Recipes of the World* presents a comprehensive look into the dietary lifestyles of many of the world's people. Published in four volumes, entries are arranged alphabetically from Algeria to Zimbabwe. Several countries—notably Australia, Brazil, Canada, and the United States—feature entries for specific ethnic groups or regions with distinctive food and recipe customs.

*Junior Worldmark Encyclopedia of Foods and Recipes of the World* features more than 700 recipes in 70 entries representing 57 countries. In selecting the countries, culture groups, and regions to include, librarian advisors were consulted. In response to suggestions from these advisors, the editors compiled the list of entries to be developed. The editors sought, with help from the advisors, to balance the contents to cover the major food customs of the world. Countries were selected from Africa (Algeria, Cameroon, Cote d'Ivoire, Ethiopia, Ghana, Kenya, Liberia, Morocco, Mozambique, Nigeria, South Africa, Tanzania, Zimbabwe); Asia (China, India, Indonesia, Japan, Korea, the Philippines, Thailand, Vietnam); the Caribbean (Cuba, Haiti, Jamaica); Europe (Czech Republic, France, Germany, Greece, Hungary, Ireland, Italy, Kazakhstan, Poland, Russia, Slovenia, Spain, Sweden, Turkey, Ukraine, United Kingdom); Central America (Guatemala);

the Middle East (Egypt, Iran, Iraq, Israel, Lebanon, Pakistan, Saudi Arabia); North America (Canada, Mexico, and the United States); Oceania (Australia, Islands of the Pacific); and South America (Argentina, Brazil, Chile, Peru).

For the United States entry, the advisors suggested preparing an innovative combination of five regional entries (including Great Lakes, Midwest, Northeast, Southern, and Western) and five ethnic/culture group entries (African American, Amish and Pennsylvania Dutch, Jewish American, Latino American, and Native American). Researchers interested in other major American ethnic and cultural groups, such as Chinese American, German American, and Lebanese American, are directed to the entries for the home countries of origin (such as China, Germany, and Lebanon).

Recipes were selected to reflect traditional national dishes as well as modern lifestyles. Persons familiar with the cuisines of the countries were consulted to ensure authenticity. The editors acknowledge the invaluable advice of these individuals, without whose help this encyclopedia would not be as authoritative: Thelma Barer-Stein; Stefanie Bruno; staff of Corky and Lenny's delicatessen, Beachwood, Ohio; Terry Hong; Marcia Hope; Solange Lamamy; staff of Middle East Restaurant, Cleveland, Ohio;

staff of Pearl of the Orient, Shaker Heights, Ohio, John Ranahan, Christine Ritsma, and Nawal Slaoui.

## Profile Features

This new addition to the *Junior Worldmark* series follows the trademark format of the *Junior Worldmark* design by organizing each entry according to a standard set of headings.

This format has been designed to allow students to compare two or more nations in a variety of ways. Also helpful to students are the translations of hundreds of foreign-language terms (which can be found in italics throughout the text) to English. Pronunciations are provided for many unfamiliar words.

Every profile contains two maps: the first displaying the nation and its location in the world, and the second presenting the nation's major cities and neighboring countries. Each entry begins with a recipe table of contents guiding the student to specific page numbers.

Most entries feature approximately ten recipes, including appetizers, main dishes, side dishes, beverages, desserts, and snacks. Recipes were selected to balance authenticity and ease of preparation. Wherever possible the recipes use easy-to-find ingredients and familiar cooking techniques. Recipes are presented with the list of ingredients first, followed by the directions in a numbered procedure list. The editors tested the recipes for most of the more than 700 dishes included in the work, and photographed steps in the procedure for many of them.

A complete glossary of cooking terms used in the entries, from allspice to zest, is included at the front of each volume.

*The body of each country's profile is arranged in seven numbered headings as follows:*

**1 GEOGRAPHIC SETTING AND ENVIRONMENT.** Location, fertile/non-fertile areas, climate (temperature and rainfall), total area, and topography (including major rivers, bodies of water, deserts, and mountains), are discussed. Various plants (including crops) and animals may also be mentioned.

**2 HISTORY AND FOOD.** The influences of early cultures, outside influences (such as explorers and colonists), and the origins of staple foods and preparation techniques are discussed. Historical dietary influences between various ethnic or religious groups may also be discussed.

**3 FOODS OF THE (COUNTRY OR CULTURE GROUP).** Foods and beverages that comprise the staples of the country's daily diet, including national dishes, are presented. Identifies foods by social class and ethnic group, where applicable. May also discuss differences between rural and urban mealtime practices.

**4 FOOD FOR RELIGIOUS AND HOLIDAY CELEBRATIONS.** Discusses dietary guidelines, restrictions, and customs for national secular and religious holidays, both in food and food preparation. Origins of holiday traditions may also be discussed. Traditional holiday menus for many holidays are presented.

**5 MEALTIME CUSTOMS.** Customs related to consumption of food at home, at restaurants, and from street vendors; entertainment of guests for a meal; number and typical times of meals; and typical school lunches and favorite snacks are discussed.

**6 POLITICS, ECONOMICS, AND NUTRITION.** Statistics from international organizations, including the United Nations and the World Bank. Discussion of health status of the population, with a focus on nutrition of the nation's children. Food laws and current dietary issues are discussed, where applicable.

**7 FURTHER STUDY.** An alphabetical list of books and web sites. Web sites were selected based on authority of hosting agency and accessibility and appropriateness for student researchers. Each web site lists when the site was last accessed. A few entries include listings of feature films notable for the role food and/or dining played in the story.

Volume 4 contains a cumulative index that provides easy access to the recipes by title and menu category (appetizers, beverages, bread, soup, main dish, side dish, snacks, vegetables, cookies and sweets, and desserts).

## Acknowledgments

Special acknowledgement goes to the many contributors who created *Junior Worldmark Encyclopedia of Foods and Recipes of the World.*

## Sources

Due to the broad scope of this encyclopedia, many sources were consulted in compiling the descriptions and recipes presented in these volumes. Of great importance were cookbooks, as well as books dedicated to the foods of a specific nation or culture group. Travel guides, where food specialties are often described for a country, were instrumental in the initial research for each entry. Cooking and lifestyle magazines, newspaper articles, and interviews with subject-matter experts and restaurateurs were also utilized. Publications of the World Bank and United Nations provided up-to-date statistics on the overall health and nutritional status of the world's children.

## Advisors

The following persons served as advisors to the editors and contributors of this work. The advisors were consulted in the early planning stages, and their input was invaluable in shaping the content and structure of this encyclopedia. Their insights, opinions, and suggestions led to many enhancements and improvements in the presentation of the material.

Elaine Fort Weischedel, Franklin Public Library, Franklin, Massachusetts

Linda Wadleigh, Media Specialist, Oconee County Middle School, Watkinsville, Georgia

Mary Mueller, Librarian, Rolla Junior High School, Rolla, Missouri

Susan A. Swain, Cuyahoga County Public Library, Ohio

## Comments and Suggestions

We welcome your comments on the *Junior Worldmark Encyclopedia of Foods and Recipes of the World*. Please write to: Editors, *Junior Worldmark Encyclopedia of Foods and Recipes of the World*, U•X•L, 27500 Drake Road, Farmington Hills, Michigan 48331-3535; call toll-free: 1-800-877-4253; or send e-mail via www.galegroup.com.

# Measurements and Conversions

In *Junior Worldmark Encyclopedia of Foods and Recipes of the World,* measurements are provided in standard U.S. measurements. The tables and conversions below are provided to help the user understand measurements typically used in cooking; and to convert quantities and cooking temperatures to metric, use these equivalents.

**Note:** The system used in the United Kingdom, referred to as UK or British, is not described here and is not referred to in this work, but educated readers may encounter this system in their research. The British cup is 10 ounces, while the U.S. is 8 ounces; the British teaspoon and tablespoon are also slightly larger than those in the United States.

## U.S. measurement equivalents

Pinch is less than a teaspoon.

Dash is a few drops or one or two shakes of a shaker.

3 teaspoons = 1 Tablespoon

2 Tablespoons = 1 liquid ounce

4 Tablespoons = ¼ cup

8 Tablespoons = ½ cup

16 Tablespoons = 1 cup

2 cups = 1 pint

2 pints = 1 quart

4 cups = 1 quart

4 quarts = 1 gallon

## Liquid measurement conversions from U.S. to metric

1 teaspoon = 5 milliliters

1 Tablespoon = 15 milliliters

1 U.S. cup = about ¼ liter (0.237 liters)

1 U.S. pint = about ½ liter (0.473 liters)

1 U.S. quart = about 1 liter (1.101 liters)

## Solid measurement conversions from U.S. to metric

1 U.S. ounce = 30 grams

1 U.S. pound = 454 grams

Butter: 7 Tablespoons = about 100 grams

Flour: 11 Tablespoons = about 100 grams

Sugar: 11 Tablespoons = about 100 grams

## Oven temperatures

Fahrenheit equals Centigrade (Celsius)

250°F = 121°C

300°F = 150°C

325°F = 164°C

350°F = 177°C

375°F = 191°C

400°F = 205°C

425°F = 219°C

450°F = 232°C

500°F = 260°C

# Getting Started with Cooking

Cooking is easier and the results are better if you take some time to learn about techniques, ingredients, and basic equipment.

## TECHNIQUES

There are three important rules to follow when using any recipe:

*First,* be clean. Always start with very clean hands and very clean utensils. Keep your hair tied back or wear a bandana.

*Second,* keep your food safe. Don't leave foods that can spoil out longer than absolutely necessary. Use the refrigerator, or pack your food with ice in a cooler if it will be cooked or eaten away from home.

*Third,* keep yourself safe. Always have an adult help when using the stove. Never try to do something else while food is cooking. Keep burners and the oven turned off when not in use.

In addition to these rules, here are some helpful tips.

*Read through* the recipe before starting to cook.

*Get out* all the utensils you will need for the recipe.

*Assemble* all the ingredients.

*Wash up* as you go to keep the cooking area tidy and to prevent foods and ingredients from drying and sticking to the utensils.

*If food burns* in the pan, fill the pan with cold water. Add a Tablespoon of baking soda and heat gently. This will help to loosen the stuck-on food.

If you follow these three rules and helpful tips—and use common sense and ask for advice when you don't understand something—cooking will be a fun activity to enjoy alone or with friends.

The basic techniques used in the recipes in *Junior Worldmark Encyclopedia of Foods and Recipes of the World* are described briefly below.

**Baking.** To cook in the oven in dry heat. Cakes and breads are baked. Casseroles are also baked. When meat is prepared in the oven, cooks may use the term "roasting" instead of baking.

**Basting.** To keep foods moist while cooking. Basting is done by spooning or brushing liquids, such as juices from the cooking pan, a marinade, or melted butter, over the food that is being cooked.

**Beating.** To mix ingredients together using a brisk stirring motion. Beating is often done using an electric mixer.

**Boiling.** To heat a liquid until bubbles appear on its surface. Many recipes ask that you bring the liquid to a boil and then lower the heat to simmer. Simmering is when the surface of the liquid is just moving slightly, with just a few bubbles now and then around the edges of the liquid.

**Chopping and cutting.** To prepare food for cooking by making the pieces smaller. To chop, cut the food in half, then quarters, and continue cutting until the cutting board is covered with smaller pieces of the food. Arrange them in a single layer, and hold the top of the chopping knife blade with both hands. Bring the knife straight up and down through the food. Turn the cutting board to cut in different directions. To dice, cut the food first into slices, and then cut a grid pattern to make small cubes of the food to be cooked. To slice, set the food on a cutting board and press the knife straight down to remove a thin section.

**Dusting with flour.** Sprinkle a light coating of flour over a surface. A sifter or sieve may be used, or flour may be sprinkled using just your fingers.

**Folding.** To stir very gently to mix together a light liquid and a heavier liquid. Folding is done with a rubber spatula, using a motion that cuts through and turns over the two liquids.

**Greasing or buttering a baking dish or cookie sheet.** To smear the surfaces with butter or shortening (or sometimes to spray with nonstick cooking spray) to prevent the food from sticking during cooking.

**Kneading.** Working with dough to prepare it to rise. First dust the surface (countertop or cutting board) with flour. Press the dough out into a flattened ball. Fold the ball in half, press down, turn the dough ball one-quarter turn, and fold and press

again. Repeat these steps, usually for 5 to 10 minutes.

**Separating eggs.** To divide an egg into two parts, the white and the yolk. This is done by cracking the egg over a bowl, and then carefully allowing the white to drip into the bowl. The yolk is transferred back and forth between the two shell halves as the whites drip down. There must be no yolk, not even a speck, in the white if the whites are to be used in a recipe. The yolk keeps the whites from beating well.

**Turning out.** To remove from the pan or bowl.

## INGREDIENTS

A trip to the grocery store can be overwhelming if you don't have a good shopping list. Cooking foods from other countries and cultures may require that you shop for unfamiliar ingredients, so a list is even more important.

### Sources for ingredients

Most of the ingredients used in the recipes in *Junior Worldmark Encyclopedia of Foods and Recipes of the World* are available in large supermarkets. If you have trouble finding an ingredient, you will need to be creative in investigating the possibilities in your area. The editors are not recommending or endorsing any specific markets or mail order sources, but offer these ideas to help you locate the items you may need.

### Ethnic grocery stores

Consult the "Grocers" section of the yellow pages of your area's telephone book. If the stores are listed by ethnic group, try looking under the country name or the the region (such as Africa, the Middle East, or Asia) to find a store that might carry what you need.

## Ethnic restaurants

Ethnic restaurants may serve the dish you want to prepare, and the staff there will probably be willing to help you find the ingredients you need. They may even be willing to sell you a small order of the hard-to-find item.

## Local library

Some libraries have departments with books in other languages. The reference librarians working there are usually familiar with the ethnic neighborhoods in your city or area, since they are often interacting with the residents there.

## Regional or city magazine

Advertisements or festival listings in your area's magazine may lead you to sources of specialty food items.

## Internet and mail order

If you have time to wait for ingredients to be shipped to you, the Internet may lead you to a grocery or specialty market that will sell you what you need and ship it to you.

## BASIC EQUIPMENT

The recipes in *Junior Worldmark Encyclopedia of Foods and Recipes of the World* typically require that you have these basic items:

**Baking pans.** Many recipes require specific baking pans, such as an 8-inch square baking pan, round cake pan, 9-inch by 13-inch baking pan, or cookie sheet. Make sure you have the pan called for in the recipe before beginning.

**Knives.** Knives for cutting must be sharp to do the job properly. It is a good idea to get an adult's help with cutting and chopping.

**Measuring cups.** Measuring cups for dry ingredients are the kind that nest inside each other in a stack. To measure liquids, cooks use a clear glass or plastic measuring cup with lines drawn on the side to indicate the measurements.

**Measuring spoons.** Measuring spoons are used to measure both liquids and dry ingredients. It is important to use spoons made for measuring ingredients, and not teaspoons and tablespoons used for eating and serving food.

**Saucepans and pots.** These round pans are taller, and are generally used for cooking dishes that have more liquid, and for boiling or steaming vegetables.

**Skillets and frying pans.** These pans are shallow, round pans with long handles. They are used to cook things on top of a burner, especially things that are cooked first on one side, and then turned to cook on the other side.

**Work surface.** A very clean countertop or cutting board must be available to prepare most dishes.

# Glossary

## A

**Allspice:** A spice derived from the round, dried berry-like fruit of a West Indian allspice tree. The mildly pungent taste resembles cinnamon, nutmeg, and cloves.

**Anise seed:** A licorice-flavored seed of the Mediterranean anise herb. It is used as an ingredient in various foods, particularly cookies, cakes, and candies.

**Arugula:** An aromatic salad green with a peppery taste. It is popularly used in Italian cuisine.

## B

**Baguette:** A long and narrow loaf of French bread that is often used for sandwiches or as an accompaniment to a variety of dishes.

**Baking soda:** A fine, white powder compound often used as an ingredient in such recipes as breads and cakes to help them rise and increase in volume.

**Basil:** An aromatic herb cultivated for its leaves. It is eaten fresh or dried and is most frequently used in tomato sauces or served with mozzarella cheese. The sweet basil variety is most common.

**Baste:** To moisten food periodically with liquid while cooking, such as broth or melted butter. Basting helps add flavor to food and prevents it from drying out.

**Bay leaf:** A pungent, spicy leaf used in a variety of cuisines, including meats, vegetables, and soups. It is most often used in combination with other herbs, such as thyme and parsley.

**Blini:** A Russian pancake made of buckwheat flour and yeast. It is commonly served with caviar and sour cream.

**Bouillon:** A clear, thin broth made by simmering meat, typically beef or chicken, or vegetables in water with seasonings.

**Braise:** To cook meat or vegetables by browning in fat, then simmering in a small quantity of liquid in a covered container.

**Bratwurst:** A small pork sausage popular with German cuisine.

**Brisket:** A cut of meat, usually beef, from the breast of an animal. It typically needs longer to cook to become tender than other meats.

**Broil:** To cook by direct exposure to heat, such as over a fire or under a grill.

## C

**Canapé:** A cracker or a small, thin piece of bread or toast spread with cheese, meat, or relish and served as an appetizer.

**Caraway seed:** The pungent seed from the caraway herb used as a flavoring and seasoning in various foods, including desserts, breads, and liquors.

**Cassava:** A tropical, tuberous plant widely used in African, Latin American, and Asian cuisines. It is most commonly used to make starch-based foods such as bread, tapioca, and pastes. It is also known as manioc or yucca (in Spanish, *yuca*).

**Charcoal brazier:** A metal pan for holding burning coals or charcoal over which food is grilled.

**Cheesecloth:** A coarse or fine woven cotton cloth that is often used for straining liquids, mulling spices, and lining molds.

**Chili:** A spicy pepper of varying size and color. It is most frequently used to add a fiery flavor to foods.

**Cilantro:** A lively, pungent herb widely used in Asian, Caribbean, and Latin American cuisines as a seasoning or garnish. It is also known as coriander.

**Citron:** A large, lemon-like fruit with a thick aromatic rind, which is commonly candied and used in desserts such as fruitcakes.

**Clove:** A fragrant spice made from the dried, woody flower bud of an evergreen tree native to tropical climates. In Indonesia, where cloves are grown, cigarettes are made from the crushed buds. Cloves also describe a single bud of garlic, shallot, or other bulb root vegetable.

**Colander:** A simple piece of kitchen equipment that resembles a metal bowl with holes in it. It is used to drain foods, such as pasta or vegetables, that have been cooked in boiling water (or other liquid).

**Coriander:** See cilantro.

**Cream of tartar:** A fine, white powder that is added to candy and frosting mixtures for a creamier consistency, or added to egg whites before being beaten to improve stability and volume.

**Cumin:** An herb cultivated for its aromatic, nut-flavored seeds. It is often used to make curries or chili powders.

**Currant:** A raisin-like colored berry that is commonly used in jams and jellies, syrups, desserts, and beverages.

# D

**Daikon:** A large, Asian radish with a sweet flavor. It is often used in raw salads, stir-fry, or shredded for a garnish.

**Dashi:** A clear soup stock, usually with a fish or vegetable base. It is frequently used in Japanese cooking.

**Double boiler:** Two pots formed to fit together, with one sitting part of the way inside the other, with a single lid fitting on both pans. The lower pot is used to hold simmering water, which gently heats the mixture in the upper pot. Foods such as custards, chocolate, and various sauces are commonly cooked this way.

# F

**Fermentation:** A process by which a food goes through a chemical change caused by enzymes produced from bacteria, microorganisms, or yeasts. It alters the appearance and/or flavor of foods and beverages such as beer, wine, cheese, and yogurt.

## G

**Garlic:** A pungent, onion-like bulb consisting of sections called cloves. The cloves are often minced or crushed and used to add sharp flavor to dishes.

**Garnish:** To enhance in appearance and/or flavor by adding decorative touches, such as herbs sprinkled on top of soup.

**Gingerroot:** A gnarled and bumpy root with a peppery sweet flavor and a spicy aroma. Asian and Indian cuisines typically use freshly ground or grated ginger as a seasoning, while Americans and Europeans tend to use ground ginger in recipes, particularly in baked goods.

## J

**Jalapeno:** A very hot pepper typically used to add pungent flavor. It is often used as a garnish or added to sauces.

**Julienne:** Foods that have been cut into thin strips, such as potatoes.

## K

**Kale:** Although a member of the cabbage family, the large leaves do not form a head. Its mild cabbage flavor is suitable in a variety of salads.

**Knead:** To mix or shape by squeezing, pressing, or rolling mixture with hands. Bread is typically prepared this way before baking.

## L

**Leek:** As part of the onion family, it has a mild and more subtle flavor than the garlic or onion. It is commonly used in salads and soups.

**Lemongrass:** Long, thin, grayish-green leaves that have a sour lemon flavor and smell. Popular in Asian (particularly Thai) cuisine, it is commonly used to flavor tea, soups, and other dishes.

## M

**Mace:** The outer membrane of the nutmeg seed. It is typically sold ground and is used to flavor a variety of dishes.

**Manioc:** See cassava.

**Marinate:** To soak a food, such as meat or vegetables, in a seasoned liquid for added flavor or to tenderize.

**Marzipan:** A sweet mixture of almond paste, sugar, and egg whites, often molded into various shapes.

**Matzo meal:** Ground unleavened (flat), brittle bread often used to thicken soups or for breading foods to be fried. It is widely popular in Jewish cuisine.

**Mince:** To cut or chop into very small pieces, typically used to prepare foods with strong flavors, such as garlic and onion.

**Mint:** A pungent herb that adds a refreshing and sweet flavor to a variety of dishes, either dried and ground or fresh. Peppermint and spearmint are the most common of over thirty varieties.

**Miso:** A thick, fermented paste made of cooked soybeans, salt, and rice or barley. A basic flavoring of Japanese cuisine, it is frequently used in making soups and sauces.

**Molasses:** A thick syrup produced in refining raw sugar or sugar beets. It ranges from light to dark brown in color and is often used as a pancake or waffle topping or a flavoring, such as in gingerbread.

# N

**Napa:** A round head of cabbage with thin, crisp, and mild-flavored leaves. It is often eaten raw or sautéed. Also known as Chinese cabbage.

# O

**Okra:** Green pods that are often used to thicken liquids and to add flavor. It is commonly used throughout the southern United States in such popular dishes as gumbo, a thick stew.

**Olive oil:** Oil derived from the pressing of olives. Varieties are ranked on acidity. Extra virgin olive oil is the least acidic and is typically the most expensive of the varieties.

**Oregano:** A strong, pungent herb commonly used in tomato-based dishes, such as pizza.

# P

**Parchment paper:** A heavy, grease- and moisture-resistant paper used to line baking pans, wrap foods, and make disposable pastry bags.

**Parsley:** A slightly peppery, fresh-flavored herb that is most commonly used as a flavoring or garnish to a wide variety of dishes. There are over thirty varieties of parsley.

**Pâté:** A seasoned meat paste made from finely minced meat, liver, or poultry.

**Peking sauce:** A thick, sweet and spicy reddish-brown sauce commonly used in Chinese cuisine. It is made of soybeans, peppers, garlic, and a variety of spices. Also known as hoisin sauce.

**Persimmon:** Edible only when fully ripe, the fruit resembles a plum in appearance. It has a creamy texture with a sweet flavor and is often eaten whole or used in such foods as puddings and various baked goods.

**Pimiento:** A sweet pepper that is often finely diced and used to stuff green olives.

**Pinto bean:** A type of mottled kidney bean that is commonly grown in the southwest United States and in Spanish-speaking countries, including Mexico. It is often used to make refried beans.

**Pistachio nut:** Commonly grown in California, the Mediterranean, and the Middle East, the mild-flavored green nut is enclosed in a hard, tan shell. They are either eaten directly out of the shell or are used to flavor a variety of dishes.

**Plantain:** A tropical fruit widely eaten in African, Caribbean, and South American cuisines. Plantains may be prepared by frying, boiling, steaming, or baking. Although closely resembling a banana, it turns black when ripe and may be eaten at any stage of ripeness.

**Prosciutto:** A seasoned, salt-cured, and air-dried ham. Eaten either cooked or raw, it is often thinly sliced and eaten with a variety of foods such as melons, figs, vegetables, or pasta.

# R

**Ramekin:** A small individual baking dish typically made of porcelain or earthenware.

**Ramen:** A Japanese dish of noodles in a broth, often garnished with pieces of meat and vegetables. An instant-style of this noodle dish is sold in individual servings in supermarkets.

# S

**Saffron:** A golden-colored spice used to add flavor or color to a wide variety of dishes. It is very expensive, so it is typically used sparingly.

**Sage:** A native Mediterranean pungent herb with grayish-green leaves. Its slightly bitter and light mint taste is commonly used in dishes containing pork, cheese, and beans, and in poultry and game stuffings.

**Sake:** A Japanese wine typically served warm in porcelain cups. The sweet, low-level alcohol sake is derived from fermented rice and does not require aging.

**Saltimbocca:** Finely sliced veal sprinkled with sage and topped with a thin slice of prosciutto. It is sautéed in butter, then braised in white wine.

**Sashimi:** A Japanese dish consisting of very thin bite-size slices of fresh raw fish, traditionally served with soy sauce, wasabi, gingerroot, or daikon radish.

**Sauerkraut:** Shredded cabbage fermented with salt and spices. It was first eaten by the Chinese, but quickly became a European (particularly German) favorite. It is popular in casseroles, as a side dish, and in sandwiches.

**Sauté:** To lightly fry in an open, shallow pan. Onions are frequently sautéed.

**Scallion:** As part of the onion family, it closely resembles a young onion before the development of the white bulb, although its flavor is slightly milder. It is often chopped and used in salads and soups.

**Shallot:** A member of the onion family that closely resembles cloves of garlic, covered in a thin, paper-like skin. It has a mild onion flavor and is used in a variety of dishes for flavoring.

**Shortening, vegetable:** A solid fat made from vegetable oils such as soybean or cottonseed oils. It is flavorless and is used in baking and cooking.

**Sieve:** A typically round device used to strain liquid or particles of food through small holes in the sieve. It is also known as a strainer.

**Simmer:** To gently cook food in a liquid at a temperature low enough to create only small bubbles that break at the liquid's surface. Simmering is more gentle than boiling the liquid.

**Skewer:** A long, thin, pointed rod made of metal or wood used to hold meat and/or vegetables in place while cooking. They are most commonly used to make shish kebabs.

**Soybean:** A generally bland-flavored bean widely recognized for its nutritive value. It is often cooked or dried to be used in salads, soups, or casseroles, as well as in such products as soy sauce, soybean oil, and tofu.

**Star anise:** A pungent and slightly bitter tasting seed that is often ground and used to flavor teas in Asian cuisines. In Western cultures it is more often added to liquors and baked goods (such as pastries).

**Steam:** A method of cooking in which food (often vegetables) is placed on a rack or in a special basket over boiling or simmering water in a covered pan. Steaming helps to retain the flavor, shape and texture, and vitamins and minerals of food better than boiling.

**Stir-fry:** A dish prepared by quickly frying small pieces of food in a large pan over very high heat while constantly and briskly stirring the ingredients until cooked. Stir-fry, which is often prepared in a special dish called a wok, is most associated with Asian cuisines.

**Stock:** The strained liquid that is the result of cooking vegetables, meat, or fish and other seasoning ingredients in water. Most soups begin with stock before other ingredients are added.

**Sushi:** Fish and vegetables prepared in bite-sized portions with rice. Fish is usually raw, but may be cooked. (Shrimp is typically cooked for sushi.)

# T

**Tamarind:** A brown fruit that is about five inches long and shaped like a large, flat green bean. Inside the brittle shell, the fruit contains large seeds surrounded by juicy, acidic pulp. The pulp, sweetened, is used to make juices and syrups.

**Tapas:** Small portions of food, either hot or cold, most commonly served to accompany a drink in Spanish and Latin American bars and restaurants.

**Tarragon:** An aromatic herb known for its anise-like (licorice) flavor. It is widely used in classic French dishes including chicken, fish, vegetables, and sauces such as béarnaise.

**Tempura:** Batter-dipped, deep-fried pieces of fish or vegetables, originally a Japanese specialty. It is most often accompanied by soy sauce.

**Thyme:** A pungent herb whose flavor is often described as a combination of mint and lemon. It is most commonly associated with French cooking. Thyme is used to flavor a variety of dishes, including meats, vegetables, fish, poultry, soups, and sauces.

**Tofu:** Ground, cooked soybeans that are pressed into blocks resembling cheese. Its bland and slightly nutty flavor is popular in Asia, particularly Japan, but is increasing in popularity throughout the United States due to its nutritive value. It may be used in soups, stir-fry, and casseroles, or eaten alone.

# V

**Vinegar:** Clear liquid made by bacterial activity that converts fermented liquids such as wine, beer, or cider into a weak solution of acetic acid, giving it a very sour taste. It can also be derived from a variety of fermented foods such as apples, rice, and barley and is most popular in Asian cuisines in sauces and marinades.

**Vinegar, rice:** Vinegar derived from fermented rice that is often used in sweet-and-sour dishes, as a salad dressing, or as a table condiment. It is generally milder than other types of vinegar.

# W

**Water bath:** A small baking pan or casserole dish placed in a larger roasting pan or cake pan to which water has been added. The small pan sits in a "bath" of water in the oven while baking. The water tempers the oven's heat, preventing the contents of the small pan from cooking too quickly.

**Whisk:** A kitchen utensil consisting of several looped wires, typically made of stainless steel, that are joined together at a handle. It is used to whip ingredients, such as eggs, creams, and sauces.

**Wok:** A large, round metal pan used for stir-fry, braising, and deep-frying, most often for Asian dishes. Most woks are made of steel or sheet iron and have two large handles on each side. It is used directly on the burner, similar to a saucepan.

**Worcestershire sauce:** A thin, dark sauce used to season meats, soups, and vegetable juices, most often as a condiment. Garlic, soy sauce, vinegar, molasses, and tamarind are just a few ingredients that may be included.

# Y

**Yucca:** See cassava.

# Z

**Zest:** The thin outer layer of the rind of a citrus fruit, particularly of an orange, grapefruit, lemon, or lime. The zest is the colorful layer of the rind, while the pith is the white portion. Most commonly used for its acidic, aromatic oils to season foods, zest can also be candied or used in pastries or desserts.

Junior
Worldmark
Encyclopedia of

# Foods and Recipes of the World

# Algeria

## *Recipes*

Saffron and Raisin Couscous with Fresh Mint................. 2

Fresh Sweet Dates ........................................................ 3

Etzai (Mint Tea)............................................................ 4

Sahlab........................................................................... 4

Banadura Salata B'Kizbara (Salad) ............................... 5

Sweet Couscous Dessert............................................... 5

Stuffed Dates and Walnuts .......................................... 6

Algerian Cooked Carrot Salad....................................... 7

Chlada Fakya (Fresh Fruit Medley).............................. 8

Cucumber & Yogurt Soup............................................. 8

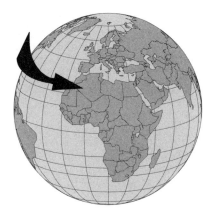

## 1 GEOGRAPHIC SETTING AND ENVIRONMENT

Algeria is located in North Africa on the Mediterranean Sea. The fertile and mountainous northern region is home to the olive tree, cork oak, and vast evergreen forests where boars and jackals roam. Fig, agave, and various palm trees grow in the warmer areas. The grape vine is native to the coastal plain. Central Algeria consists of the High Plateaus that contain salt marshes and dry or shallow salt lakes. The land becomes more arid (dry) the farther south one travels, eventually becoming the Sahara Desert. Roughly 80 percent of the country is desert, where vegetation is sparse. Camels are widely used in this arid region, although jackals, rabbits, scorpions, and snakes also occupy the deserts.

The coastal region has a typical Mediterranean climate—pleasant nearly year round, with winter temperatures rarely falling below freezing (32ºF). Rainfall is also abundant along the coast. Farther inland, higher altitudes receive considerable frost and occasional snow. Little or no rainfall occurs throughout the summer months in this region. In the Sahara Desert, rainfall is unpredictable and unevenly distributed.

## 2 HISTORY AND FOOD

Algerian cuisine traces its roots to various countries and ancient cultures that once ruled, visited, or traded with the country. Berber tribesmen were one of the country's earliest inhabitants. Their arrival, which may extend as far back as 30,000 B.C., marked the beginning of wheat cultivation, *smen* (aged, cooked butter), and fruit consumption, such as dates. The introduction of semolina wheat by the Carthaginians (who occupied much of northern Africa) led the

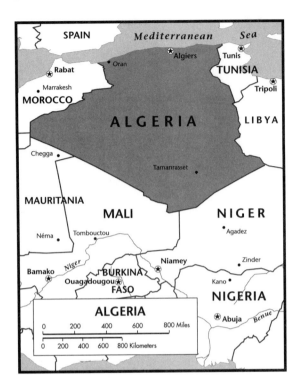

across the Mediterranean from Spain during an invasion in the 1500s. Sweet pastries from the Turkish Ottomans and tea from European traders also made their way into Algerian cuisine around this time.

In the early 1800s, Algerians were driven off their own lands and forced to surrender their crops and farmland to the French. The French introduced their diet and culture to the Algerians, including their well-known loaves of bread and the establishment of sidewalk cafés. This French legacy remains evident in Algerian culture. In fact, Algeria's second language is French. (Arabic is the official language.)

Tomatoes, potatoes, zucchini, and chilies, significant to Algerian local cuisine, were brought over from the New World.

Berbers to first create *couscous*, Algeria's national dish. The Romans, who eventually took over Algeria, also grew various grains. At the beginning of the twenty-first century, Algeria ranked among the top ten importers of grain (such as wheat and barley) in the world, according to ArabicNews.com.

Muslim Arabs invaded Algeria in the 600s, bringing exotic spices such as saffron, nutmeg, ginger, cloves, and cinnamon from the Spice Islands of eastern Indonesia. They also introduced the Islamic religion to the Berbers. Islam continues to influence almost every aspect of an Algerian's life, including the diet.

Olives (and olive oil) and fruits such as oranges, plums, and peaches were brought

## Saffron and Raisin Couscous with Fresh Mint

### Ingredients

2 cups water

½ teaspoon saffron

1 teaspoon extra virgin olive oil

½ teaspoon salt

2 cups couscous

¼ cup raisins

3 Tablespoons fresh mint, chopped

### Procedure

1. In a saucepan, bring the 2 cups of water to a boil and add the saffron.

2. Remove from the heat, cover, and let stand for 30 minutes.

3. Return the pan to the heat, return to a boil, and mix in the olive oil, salt, couscous, and raisins.

4. Remove from the heat, cover, and let stand for 30 minutes.

5. Top with the fresh mint.

Makes 8 servings.

∞

## *Fresh Sweet Dates*

### Ingredients

1 pound fresh dates

½ cup butter

¾ cup flour

1 teaspoon cardamom, ground

### Procedure

1. Remove the pits from the dates and arrange in 6 individual serving dishes.

2. Melt the butter in a heavy saucepan and stir in the flour.

3. Cook over medium heat, stirring constantly, until the flour turns golden brown. Be careful not to burn.

4. Remove the flour mixture from the heat and stir in the cardamom.

5. Remove from heat and allow to cool slightly, stirring occasionally.

6. While still warm, pour over the warm dates and allow to cool to room temperature before serving.

Makes 6 servings.

## 3 FOODS OF THE ALGERIANS

Traditional Algerian cuisine, a colorful combination of Berber, Turkish, French, and Arab tastes, can be either extremely mild or packed with flavorful seasonings. Ginger, saffron, onion, garlic, coriander, cumin, cinnamon, parsley, and mint are essential in any Algerian pantry.

*Couscous*, the national dish, is often mistaken as a grain itself, rather than pasta. The pasta dough is a mixture of water and coarse, grainy semolina wheat particles. The dough is then crumbled through a sieve to create tiny pellets. Algerians prefer lamb, chicken, or fish to be placed on a bed of warm couscous, along with cooked vegetables such as carrots, chickpeas, and tomatoes, and spicy stews. Couscous can also be used in desserts by adding a variety of ingredients, such as cinnamon, nutmeg, dates, and figs.

No Algerian meal would be complete without bread, normally a long, French loaf. Similar to Middle Eastern customs, bread is often used to scoop food off of a plate or to soak up a spicy sauce or stew. More traditional Berber families usually eat flat, wheat bread.

*Mechoui*, a roasted whole lamb cooked on an outdoor spit, is usually prepared when a large group of people gathers together. The animal is seasoned with herb butter so the skin is crispy and the meat inside is tender and juicy. Bread and various dried fruits and vegetables, including dates (whose trees can thrive in the country's Sahara desert), often accompany *mechoui*.

Beverages such as mint tea are a favorite among all North African countries. Tea is usually offered to visiting guests, though coffee flavored with cardamom is another option. With the abundance of fruits year round, fresh juices are plentiful and children tend to favor apricot nectar. *Sharbats*, fruit or nut-flavored milk drinks, are popular with all ages, including *sahlab*, a sweet, milky drink. Traditional Berbers, in particular, prefer drinks made from goat milk, although cow milk is now available. *Basbousa* (Egyptian semolina cake), *tamina* (roasted semolina with butter and honey), and sweetened *couscous* are just a few sweets enjoyed by the Algerians.

EPD Photos/Sana Abed-Kotob

*Sahlab, shown topped with chopped pistachios, is a favorite treat, often served when the weather is chilly.*

∞

## Etzai (Mint Tea)

### Ingredients

1½ Tablespoons green tea

Boiling water

3 Tablespoons sugar, or to taste

Handful of fresh mint leaves

### Procedure

1. Put the tea in a teapot.
2. Pour in a cupful of boiling water, then immediately pour it out again. This is to wash the leaves.
3. Add the sugar to taste, then the mint leaves.
4. Pour in boiling water 12 inches away from the top (this oxygenates the tea) and stir well. Be extremely careful not to splash the boiling water.
5. Serve the tea very hot, again pouring it from a height of about 12 inches.

∞

## Sahlab

### Ingredients

3 cups (8 ounces each) milk

1 cup sugar

½ cup cornstarch

¾ cup water

¼ cup raisins

¼ cup coconut

¼ cup walnuts or pistachios, chopped

1 teaspoon cinnamon

### Procedure

1. In a small mixing bowl, dissolve the cornstarch in the water and set aside.
2. In a heavy saucepan, bring the milk to a boil over low to medium heat.
3. As soon as the milk boils, reduce the heat.
4. Stir in the sugar, and allow the milk to simmer until the sugar has dissolved (no more than 1 minute).
5. Slowly pour the cornstarch mixture into the milk, making sure to whisk rapidly to prevent the milk from sticking to the bottom of the saucepan. The milk will gradually thicken.
6. When it reaches the consistency of a thick gravy, remove from heat.
7. Pour *sahlab* into decorative small bowls, glasses, or mugs.
8. Sprinkle with raisins, coconut, chopped nuts, and cinnamon, if desired.
9. Serve hot.

Makes 6 servings.

∽

## Banadura Salata B'Kizbara (Tomato and Coriander Salad)

### Ingredients

½ cup fresh coriander leaves, chopped

1 small hot chili pepper, seeded and finely chopped

5 medium ripe tomatoes, peeled

4 Tablespoons fresh lemon juice

¼ cup virgin olive oil

1 teaspoon salt

### Procedure

1. Slice the peeled tomatoes and place in a bowl.
2. Sprinkle the chopped coriander over the tomatoes.
3. Mix the chopped chili pepper with the lemon juice and 1 teaspoon of salt.
4. Beat the olive oil into the chili-lemon juice mixture.
5. Pour over the tomatoes and coriander.
6. Let rest 15 minutes before serving.

Makes 6 servings.

∽

## Sweet Couscous Dessert

### Ingredients

1 cup plus 2 Tablespoons couscous

⅔ cup warm water

⅔ cup fresh dates

⅔ cup ready-to-eat prunes

6 Tablespoons butter, melted

¼ cup sugar

1 teaspoon cinnamon, ground

½ teaspoon nutmeg, ground

Rose petals, to decorate (optional)

### Procedure

1. Place the couscous in a bowl and cover with ⅔ cup warm water.
2. Leave 15 minutes to plump up.
3. Halve each date lengthwise, remove the seed and cut into 4 pieces.
4. Roughly chop the prunes.
5. Fluff up the grains of couscous with a fork, then place in a cheesecloth-lined sieve and steam over simmering water for 15 minutes until hot.
6. Transfer to a bowl and fluff up again with a fork.
7. Add the melted butter, sugar, dates, and prunes.
8. Pile the couscous into a cone shape in a serving dish.
9. Mix the cinnamon and nutmeg together and sprinkle over couscous.
10. Serve decorated with rose petals, if desired.

Makes 4 servings.

## 4 FOOD FOR RELIGIOUS AND HOLIDAY CELEBRATIONS

The overwhelming majority of Algerians, about 99 percent, follow the beliefs of Islam, the country's official religion (Christians and Jews make up only 1 percent of the population).

The Algerian observance of Ramadan, the ninth month of the Islamic year (most often November or December), is the most celebrated of all holidays. During the monthlong observance, Muslims are required to fast (avoid consuming food and drink) between sunrise and sunset, although young, growing children and pregnant women may be allowed to eat a small amount. At the end of each day during Ramadan, sometimes as late as midnight,

(festival) in Tlemcen and the tomato *moussem* in Adrar.

∞

### A Typical Holiday Menu

Cucumber and yogurt soup
Stuffed dates and walnuts
Roast stuffed leg of lamb
Tomato and raisin-stuffed eggplant
Potato & chickpea salad
Cooked carrots
Fresh fruit medley

families join together for a feast. French loaves or wheat bread and a pot of hot mint tea will likely serve as refreshments.

The meal marking the end of Ramadan, *Eid al-Fitr*, is the most important feast. It almost always begins with soup or stew. Lamb or beef is most often served as the main dish, although families living close to the Mediterranean in northern Algeria enjoy a variety of seafood. In most Algerian homes, a bowl of fresh fruit is placed on the table at the end of the meal. Traditionally, each person is responsible for peeling and slicing his or her own fruit. However, on special occasions such as *Eid al-Fitr*, the host will often serve the fruit already peeled, sliced, and flavored (most often with cinnamon and various citrus juices).

Other popular holiday celebrations are Labor Day (May 1), and the anniversary of the revolution over French control (November 1). Two local festivals that are celebrated every spring are the cherry *moussem*

∞

### Stuffed Dates and Walnuts

**Ingredients**

12 fresh dates

½ cup ground almonds

2 Tablespoons pistachio nuts, very finely chopped

2 Tablespoons granulated sugar

Orange flower water (found at specialty stores)

24 walnut halves

Powdered sugar, to decorate

**Procedure**

1. With a sharp knife, make a slit down the length of each date and carefully remove the seed.

2. In a bowl, mix together the ground almonds, chopped pistachio nuts, and granulated sugar.

3. Add enough orange flower water to make a smooth paste.

4. Shape half of the paste into 12 nuggets the size of date seeds and use to stuff the dates.

5. Use the remaining paste to sandwich the walnut halves together in pairs.

6. Sift a little powdered sugar over the stuffed dates and walnuts. Serves best with rich coffee.

Makes 4 to 6 servings.

Cory Langley

*The marketplace in Algiers bustles with shoppers.*

## ∞

## Algerian Cooked Carrot Salad

### Ingredients

1 pound carrots

3 garlic cloves, chopped

Pinch of salt

Pinch of sugar

Lemon juice

¼ teaspoon salt

½ teaspoon cayenne pepper

¼ teaspoon cumin

Parsley, chopped

### Procedure

1. Scrape the carrots and cut them into four pieces lengthwise.

2. Cook in a little water with garlic and a pinch of salt and sugar for 15 minutes.

3. Drain and chill the carrots.

4. Just before serving, cover with lemon juice, about ¼ teaspoon of salt, cayenne pepper, and cumin.

5. Sprinkle with chopped parsley.

Makes 6 servings.

∞

## Chlada Fakya
## (Fresh Fruit Medley)

### Ingredients

½ cantaloupe, peeled, seeded, cut into bite-sized pieces

½ honeydew melon, peeled, seeded, cut into bite-sized pieces

1 cup strawberries, cut in half, stemmed, washed

2 bananas, peeled and thinly sliced

5 seedless oranges, peeled and thinly sliced

½ cup orange juice

Juice of 2 lemons

2 Tablespoons sugar

1 teaspoon vanilla extract

1 teaspoon cinnamon

### Procedure

1. In medium serving bowl, carefully toss cantaloupe, honeydew melon, strawberries, bananas, and oranges.

2. In a small bowl, mix orange and lemon juice, sugar, vanilla, and cinnamon, and pour over fruit.

3. Toss gently, and refrigerate until ready to serve (at the end of a holiday feast, for example). Toss again before serving in individual bowls.

Makes 6 servings.

∞

## Cucumber & Yogurt Soup

### Ingredients

1 large cucumber

2½ cups plain yogurt

2 cloves garlic, crushed

1 lemon rind, finely grated

2 Tablespoons fresh mint, chopped

Salt and freshly ground black pepper

⅔ cup ice water

Mint leaves, to garnish

### Procedure

1. Rinse the cucumber and trim the ends. Do not peel.

2. Grate the cucumber into a bowl.

3. Stir in the yogurt, garlic, lemon rind, and chopped mint.

4. Season well with salt and pepper.

5. Cover the bowl and chill 1 hour.

6. Stir in ⅔ cup ice water. Add more water if the soup seems a little thick.

7. Adjust the seasoning, then pour into chilled soup bowls.

8. Garnish with mint leaves.

Makes 6 servings.

## 5 MEALTIME CUSTOMS

Arabs are hospitable and encourage family and friends to share their food. Even an unexpected visitor will be greeted warmly and offered coffee (often flavored with cardamom), while the females of the household prepare the meal. Cooking continues to be considered a woman's duty, as it has in the past. Historically, recipes and cooking customs have been passed down through generations by word of mouth when women gather together to prepare meals.

All meals (normally three a day) are leisurely and sociable, although there are varying degrees of structure and etiquette (polite behavior). Seated at a low table (*tbla* or *mida*), food is traditionally eaten with the

*The traditional after-dinner treat consists of a platter of fresh fruit topped with domestically grown sweet dates.*

thumb, forefinger, and middle finger of the right hand (the left hand is considered unclean). To use four or five fingers is considered to be a sign of over-eating and should be avoided. The dining atmosphere in a middle class family may be a bit more elegant. A servant or young family member might visit each individual at the table, offering a bowl of perfumed water to diners for washing their hands before the meal is eaten.

The country's capital, Algiers, and popular coastal towns tend to have a wide variety of restaurants, particularly French, Italian, and Middle Eastern cuisine. Southern Algeria is less populated, and is farther from Algiers and the Mediterranean waters, where seafood and the hustle and bustle of trade are plentiful. Menus usually begin with either a soup or salad, followed by roast meat (usually lamb or beef) or fish as a main course, with fresh fruit commonly completing the meal. In the towns, *souks* (markets) or street stalls offer take-home products, such as spicy *brochettes* (kebabs) on French bread for those on the run. With the exception of an occasional fast food burger, school lunches are often such traditional foods as couscous, dried fruit, stews, and sweet fruit drinks.

## 6 POLITICS, ECONOMICS, AND NUTRITION

Malnutrition has been one of the principal health problems in Algeria in recent years. About 5 percent of the population of Algeria is classified as undernourished by the World Bank. This means they do not receive adequate nutrition in their diet. Of children under the age of five, about 13 percent are underweight, and nearly 18 percent are stunted (short for their age). Very little land in Algeria is cultivated (only 3 percent), too little for the country to be self-sufficient and feed its own people.

However, 91 percent of the population has access to adequate sanitation: nearly 100 percent of those in urban areas and 80 percent in rural areas. Free medical care, which was introduced by the Algerian government in 1974 under the Social Security system, helps pay for those who are ill.

## 7 FURTHER STUDY

### Books

Brennan, Georgeanne. *The Mediterranean Herb Cookbook*. San Francisco, CA: Chronicle Books, 2000.

Mackley, Lesley. *The Book of North African Cooking*. New York: The Berkley Publishing Group, 1998.

Walden, Hilaire. *North African Cooking*. Edison, New Jersey: Quintet Publishing Limited, 1995.

Webb, Lois Sinaiko. *Holidays of the World Cookbook for Students*. Phoenix, AZ: The Oryx Press, 1995.

### Web Sites

ArabicNews.com. [Online] Available http://www.arabicnews.com/ (accessed March 6, 2001).

CookingLight.com. [Online] Available http://www.cooking-light.com/ (accessed March 8, 2001).

### Films

*Samia,* by Philippe Faucon. (Official selection at the 2000 Venice Film Festival) Samia is a teen-age girl of Algerian descent living in Marseille (southern France) with her family. At home, Samia and her two sisters live in an Algerian culture. They speak the language, eat Algerian food, and observe the customs of their Muslim religion. But, as youngsters, they are torn; despite their parents' objections, they want to fit in with the rest of society. To be a young girl in this environment is even more difficult because her family's traditions have society believing that she has no independence. As she begins to spread her wings, the quick-witted and attractive Samia soon finds herself in conflict with her family. (In French and Arabic with English subtitles.)

# Argentina

## Recipes

Carbonada Criolla (Stew) ............................................ 12
Chimichurri (Dipping Sauce) ..................................... 13
Empanadas (Little Meat Pies) .................................... 13
Bocaditos (Finger Sandwiches) ................................. 14
Fruit Salad with Frozen Yogurt ................................. 15
Submarino (Milk with Chocolate Syrup) ..................... 16
Dulce de Leche (Milk Jam) ........................................ 17
Alfajores de Maizena (Corn Starch Cookies) ................ 17

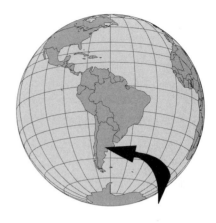

## 1 GEOGRAPHIC SETTING AND ENVIRONMENT

Argentina is a wedge-shaped country, the second largest (after Brazil) in South America. In the west, it has the Andes Mountains, but the majority of Argentina's land is low. Because Argentina lies in the Southern Hemisphere, the winter months are May through August, and the warmest summer month is January. Argentina's climate and rich, lowland regions combine to make it one of the world's greatest food-producing nations. More than 4 percent of the world's cattle are raised by Argentine cattle ranchers. Argentina is also South America's largest producer of honey, an ingredient that makes its way into many delicious Argentine desserts.

## 2 HISTORY AND FOOD

Native Indians lived in Argentina many years before the European explorers arrived. Members of an Indian tribe in the northern part of Argentina were farmers who grew squash, melons, and sweet potatoes. Span-ish settlers came to Argentina in 1536. Between 1880 and 1890, nearly one million immigrants came from Europe to live in Argentina. Most were from Italy and Spain. The Italians introduced pizza, as well as all kinds of pasta dishes, including spaghetti and lasagna. British, German, Jewish, and other immigrants also settled in Argentina, all bringing their styles of cooking and favorite foods with them. The British brought tea, starting the tradition of teatime. All of these cultures influenced the dishes of Argentina.

## 3 FOODS OF THE ARGENTINES

Beef is the national dish of Argentina. There are huge cattle ranches in Argentina, and the *gaucho,* or Argentine cowboy, is a well-known symbol of Argentine individualism. Many dishes contain meat, but prepared in different ways. A favorite main course is *parrillada,* a mixed grill of steak and other cuts of beef. Grilled steak is called *churrasco,* a beef roast cooked over an open fire is called *asado,* and beef that is

11

dipped in eggs, crumbs, and then fried is called *milanesa*. *Carbonada* is a stew that contains meat, potatoes, sweet potatoes, and chunks of corn on the cob.

✂

## Carbonada Criolla
### (Stew with Meat, Vegetables, and Fruit)

### Ingredients

3 Tablespoons olive oil

2 pounds of stewing beef, cut into 1-inch chunks

4 large tomatoes, chopped thick

1 green pepper, chopped thick

1 large onion

3 cloves garlic, minced

2 bay leaves

1 teaspoon oregano

2 cups canned chicken stock

3 potatoes, diced into 1-inch cubes

3 sweet potatoes, diced into 1-inch cubes

2 ears of corn, cut into 1-inch widths (or use 2 cups of frozen corn)

2 zucchini, diced into ½-inch pieces

2 peaches in ½-inch pieces

2 pears in ½-inch pieces

### Procedure

1. Heat oil in heavy pot.

2. Brown beef in separate batches so that all of it gets cooked. Remove from the pot and set aside.

3. In that same pot, cook tomatoes, pepper, onion, and garlic until soft.

4. Add bay leaves, oregano, and chicken stock, and bring to a boil.

5. Return beef to the pot, and add potatoes and sweet potatoes. Cover and simmer 15 minutes.

6. Stir in zucchini and corn. Simmer 10 more minutes, or until vegetables are almost soft, then add the peaches and pears.

7. Cook 5 more minutes.

8. Serve hot.

Makes 6 to 8 servings.

Because many Argentines are descendents of the Italian immigrants who came to Argentina in the late 1800s, Italian dishes are found throughout the country. Some favorite Italian dishes include pizza, all kinds of pastas (such as spaghetti and ravioli), and *ñoquis*, (gnocchi—potato dumplings) served with meat and tomato sauce.

Argentines eat more fruit than almost any other group of people in the world. Some favorite fruits include peaches, apricots, plums, pears, cherries, grapes, and *tuna*, the fruit of a prickly pear cactus.

*Empanadas*, little pies usually stuffed with beef, vegetables, and cheese, are a favorite dish. These are eaten by hand and they are often enjoyed as a snack, or may be carried to school for lunch. *Chimichurri*, a dipping sauce, is usually served with *empanadas*. Because the sauce has to sit for two hours before eating, it is prepared before the *empanadas*.

## Chimichurri (Dipping Sauce)

### Ingredients

½ cup olive oil

2 Tablespoons lemon juice

⅓ cup fresh parsley, minced

1 clove garlic

2 shallots (or 2 small onions), minced

1 teaspoon minced basil, thyme, or oregano (or mixture of these, if preferred)

Salt and pepper to taste

### Procedure

1. Combine all ingredients in a bowl and

let sit for at least 2 hours before serving with *empanadas*.

## Empanadas (Little Meat Pies)

### Ingredients

FILLING:

1 pound ground beef

½ cup onions, chopped

8 green olives, chopped

1 teaspoon salt

¼ teaspoon oregano

PASTRY:

2½ cups flour

1 egg yolk

½ cup water

¼ cup butter

1 teaspoon vinegar

½ teaspoon salt

### Procedure

FILLING:

1. Brown the ground beef and onions in a frying pan until meat has lost all its pink color.

2. Stir in the remaining ingredients.

3. Drain the mixture well, and allow it to cool.

PASTRY:

1. Preheat oven to 400°F.

2. In a bowl, mix the flour, butter, egg, yolk, and vinegar together by hand.

3. Stir the salt into the water and sprinkle water, a little at a time, over the flour mixture.

4. Knead the dough until it is smooth. (To knead, flatten the dough on a surface that has been dusted with a little flour.

## 4 FOOD FOR RELIGIOUS AND HOLIDAY CELEBRATIONS

Lent is the 40-day period preceding Easter in the Christian year. During the week before Lent, a large festival, Carnival, is celebrated in many parts of Argentina. During Carnival, people dress up in costumes and dance. They eat spicy food, including corn stew and *humitas en chala* (corn patties wrapped and cooked in their husks). It is a tradition to eat a cake in the shape of a large ring. On Easter, children eat chocolate eggs with tiny candies hidden inside.

Because it is also tradition in the Roman Catholic Church to not eat meat during Lent, Argentines eat more seafood dishes during this time. *Bocaditos* (finger sandwiches), made with shrimp are a popular lunch or snack food during Lent.

EPD Photos

*Empanadas, homemade or purchased from a vendor, are popular for lunches or as snacks.*

Fold the dough in half and flatten again. Turn. Repeat the process for about 15 minutes.)

5. For each *empanada*, roll ¼ cup of dough into a 9-inch circle.

6. Put ½ cup filling on the circle, and fold it in half.

7. Press the edges of the dough together, and poke a small hole in the top using a toothpick. Place on a cookie sheet.

8. Repeat process until all the dough and filling are used up.

9. Bake 10–15 minutes.

10. Serve hot with *chimichurri*.

## ⬨

## *Bocaditos (Finger Sandwiches)*

### Ingredients

12 thin slices French bread

1 container (3-ounce) cream cheese with chives

½ cucumber, thinly sliced

4 to 6 precooked shrimp

4 cherry tomatoes, sliced

### Procedure

1. Cut crusts off the bread.

2. Spread a thin layer of cream cheese on each slice of bread.

3. Place cucumber slices, tomatoes, and shrimp on one slice, and cover with another slice of bread to make a sandwich. (Any combination of these ingredients may be used.)

4. Cut into triangles or rectangles.

Serves 8 to 10.

On Christmas Eve, celebrated on December 24, Argentines eat a late meal of cold beef, chicken, or turkey, and fruit salad. Because Christmas occurs during summertime in South America, Argentines often eat the meal outside on decorated tables. After dinner, they eat almonds, dried fruits, and *pan dulce*, a sweet bread that is similar to fruitcake but has fewer fruits and nuts.

EPD Photos

*Fruit salad offers a refreshing balance of sweet and tart flavors with honey and lemon juice in the dressing, and a topping of sweet, light frozen yogurt.*

## ∞
## *Fruit Salad with Frozen Yogurt*

### Ingredients

3 Tablespoons honey

3 Tablespoons lemon juice

1 medium apple, cored and chopped

1 medium plum, pitted and sliced

1 large orange, peeled and sliced into ¼-inch rounds

1 large grapefruit, peeled and sectioned

1 medium banana, peeled and sliced into rounds

1 quart frozen vanilla yogurt

### Procedure

1. In a large bowl, whisk together the honey and lemon juice.

2. Stir in the fruit, and serve topped with a scoop of frozen yogurt.

In many areas of Argentina, people hold festivals to honor aspects of the environment. For example, a city on the Atlantic coast celebrates the seafood harvest that is brought in from its fishing grounds. It is tradition for people to eat a seafood feast of shrimp, crab, and scallops. After the feast, a parade with people dressed in sea-creature costumes is held. Someone dressed as The Queen of the Sea leads the parade, sitting in a giant seashell.

## 5 MEALTIME CUSTOMS

Argentine families, like families everywhere, are busy. Because everyone is on a different schedule, they aren't able to eat every meal together. *Desayuno* (day-sigh-OO-noh, breakfast) is often a light meal of rolls or bread with jam and coffee. Most working people in the cities have a small

time tradition comes from the British immigrants that brought tea to Argentina in the late 1800s.

Vendors sell food on the streets (the equivalent to "fast food"). Ice cream vendors sell *helado,* Argentine ice cream, and warm peanuts, sweet popcorn, and candied apples. Some vendors sell *choripan* (a sausage sandwich) and soda. *Empanadas*, little pies stuffed with beef, chicken, seafood, or vegetables, are a popular snack. Children can take vegetable-filled *empanadas* to school for lunch. A favorite drink is a *submarino*, or milk with chocolate syrup.

Cory Langley

*An Argentine fruit and vegetable vendor and her daughter greet customers at a market.*

comida (coh-MEE-dah, lunch) such as a pizza from a cafeteria. A farmer eats a hot dish for lunch, carried out to him in the field, of beef, potatoes, and chunks of corn-on-the-cob. Upper-class city families usually eat a large midday meal of meat, potatoes, and green vegetables.

In the late afternoon, Argentines have a snack of tea, sandwiches, and cake to hold over their appetite until dinner (*cena,* SAY-nah), typically eaten around 9 P.M. The tea-

∞

## *Submarino*
## *(Milk with Chocolate Syrup)*

### Ingredients

1 glass of cold milk

1 teaspoon chocolate syrup

### Procedure

1. Place the spoon with the syrup in the cold milk, but don't stir it.

2. Drink a little milk, then lick some of the chocolate off the spoon.

3. Continue until glass is empty.

The dinner meal has several courses, including meat dishes, and ends with dessert. *Dulce de leche* (milk jam) is a favorite dessert for many Argentine children. It is often eaten with bananas or as a filling in *alfajores* (corn starch cookies).

EPD Photos

*To make Dulce de Leche (milk jam), fill a pan with sweetened, condensed milk and cover the pan with foil. Place it in a larger pan with about one inch of water in it.*

∞

## Dulce de Leche (Milk Jam)

**Ingredients**

1 can sweetened condensed milk

**Procedure**

1. Preheat oven to 425°F.
2. Pour the sweetened condensed milk into an 8-inch round pie or square cake pan, and cover it with foil.
3. Place the pan in a shallow pan filled with one inch of water. Bake for one hour.
4. Allow to cool; eat with bananas or as a cookie filling.

∞

## Alfajores de Maizena (Corn Starch Cookies)

**Ingredients**

2½ cups cornstarch

1⅔ cups flour

½ teaspoon baking soda

2 teaspoons baking powder

¾ cup sugar

1 cup (2 sticks) butter or margarine

3 egg yolks

1 Tablespoon vanilla extract

Grated lemon peel

**Ingredients**

1. Preheat oven to 350°F.
2. Sift the cornstarch with the flour, baking soda and baking powder in a bowl.
3. Beat margarine and sugar, and add the egg yolks one at a time. Mix well.
4. Add dry ingredients a little at a time.
5. Add vanilla and lemon peel. Mix to form a stiff, elastic dough.
6. Stretch until the dough is about ½-inch thick over surface covered with flour.
7. Cut into circles using the rim of a drinking glass or a round cookie cutter and put the circles on an ungreased cookie sheet.
8. Bake for about 15 minutes. Let cool.
9. Spread some *dulce de leche* on one cookie and sandwich with another cookie, and repeat with the rest of the cookies.

## 6 POLITICS, ECONOMICS, AND NUTRITION

Most people in Argentina receive adequate nutrition in their diets, although the World Bank classifies a small percentage as malnourished. Almost three-fourths of the population has access to safe drinking water and sanitation (hygienic conditions and safe disposal of waste products). A small percent of children under age five are underweight (about 2 percent) or stunted (are short for their age, 5 percent). These children are from the poorest Argentine families, and may live in cities or rural areas.

## 7 FURTHER STUDY

### Books

*Argentina*. Boston: APA Publications, 1997.

Greenberg, Arnold. *Buenos Aires: And the Best of Argentina Alive!* Edison, NJ: Hunter Publishing, Inc., 2000.

Hintz, Martin. *Argentina*. New York: Children's Press, 1998.

Novas, Himilce and Silva, Rosemary. *Latin American Cooking Across the U.S.A.* New York: Knopf, 1997.

Parnell, Helga. *Cooking the South American Way.* Minneapolis: Lerner, 1991.

Peterson, Marge. *Argentina: A Wild West Heritage.* Parsippany, NJ: Dillon Press, 1997.

### Web Sites

Global Gourmet. [Online] Available http://www.globalgourmet.com/destinations/argentina/ (accessed March 1, 2001).

Latin American Recipes. [Online] Available http://www.ma.iup.edu/Pueblo/latino_cultures/recipes.html (accessed March 6, 2001).

Margarita's Favorite Recipes. [Online] Available http://www.lacabe.com/marga/food/recipes/alfajores.html (accessed February 24, 2001).

# Australia

## *Recipes*

Grated Carrot, Apple, and Raisin Salad ......................... 20
Australian Meat Pie ...................................................... 21
Black Australian Coffee ................................................ 22
ANZAC Biscuits ........................................................... 22
Lamingtons .................................................................. 23
Christmas Shortbread ................................................... 24
Pavlova ....................................................................... 24
Quick No-Cook Mini-Pavlova ....................................... 25
Chocolate Crackles ...................................................... 27
Toast with Vegemite or Milo Spread ............................. 27

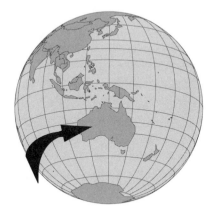

## 1 GEOGRAPHIC SETTING AND ENVIRONMENT

Australia is the world's smallest continent. Lying southeast of Asia between the Pacific and Indian oceans, its diverse landscapes and climates are home to a wide variety of plants and animals.

It is generally warm and dry all year round, with no extreme cold and little frost. Average annual rainfall is 17 inches (42 centimeters), much less than the mean for all the countries of the world of 26 inches (66 centimeters). As a result, insufficient rainfall can cause droughts that threaten to destroy crops.

The country's limited rainfall can also cause problems with water quality and availability. Because Australia produces most of its own food, a water shortage for plants and animals can cause agricultural production to suffer.

## 2 HISTORY AND FOOD

Captain Arthur Phillip of England established the first modern settlement in Australia in January 1788. The settlers were not very experienced as farmers and early agricultural practices were disastrous. Crop failure caused food shortages and even starvation. Settlers depended on goods imported from England—such as tea, flour, beef, oatmeal, and cheese—to survive. They also learned to eat foods they found around them, such as fish and wild fruits and nuts.

The Australian diet has been heavily influenced by peoples from all over the world. The Potato Famine of the 1840s in Ireland led many desperate starving Irish people to leave their homeland, seeking relief in Australia (as well as Canada, the United States, and elsewhere). Gold was discovered in Australia a few years later, bringing more people to the country. Following World War II (1939–45), Europeans and Asians arrived in greater numbers. As a

result, cuisines from other countries, such as Italy, Greece, and Lebanon, became popular. Europeans introduced tea, cocoa, coffee, fruits, and a variety of cheeses, and Asians introduced new spices and the technique of stir-fry.

## 3 FOODS OF THE AUSTRALIANS

The end of World War II brought about significant change in Australian cuisine. People from Europe and Asia brought new crops, seasonings, and cooking methods with them.

Wheat, rice, oranges, bananas, and grapes are just a few of the crops that grow in abundance throughout the country. Meat has always been a large part of the Australian diet, although Australians (like others around the world) began to be concerned about controlling cholesterol and fat in their diet, and decreased their consumption of meat slightly toward the end of the twentieth century. Kangaroo, though once a popular meat in Australia's early history, is no longer widely consumed; beef, lamb, pork, poultry, and seafood are more common in twenty-first century Australia.

∞

## Grated Carrot, Apple, and Raisin Salad

### Ingredients

1 head of lettuce

1 medium carrot, grated

1 medium red apple, chopped fine

¼ cup raisins

1 Tablespoon coconut, flaked

Juice of lemon

### Procedure

1. Carefully remove several firm leaves from the head of lettuce, and arrange in a bowl.

2. Mix the remaining ingredients in a bowl.

3. Mound mixture in the lettuce "cup." Serve with cottage cheese, chicken, or lean cold meat.

Serves 6.

A typical breakfast may consist of fruit, toast with Vegemite (a salty yeast spread), fried eggs and bacon, and juice. Lunch may be an apple or a salad (such as Grated Carrot, Apple, and Raisin salad), a sandwich filled with tuna or deli meats, and an ANZAC biscuit for a treat. (ANZAC is the acronym for Australia and New Zealand Army Corps. No one knows for sure, but many people think these biscuits were first prepared for troops—and for Australian and New Zealand families—around 1915 during World War I.) Dinnertime often brings leg of lamb or barbecued prawns (shrimp), roasted vegetables, a salad, and a custard or tart for dessert. *Damper*, a simple home-made bread, and *billy tea*, named for the pot it is heated in, both remain a staple for any meal.

Meat pie is considered the Australian national dish. One newspaper, the Sydney *Morning Herald,* reported some statistics about meat pie consumption in the country:

- Almost 260 million pies are consumed every year, or almost 15 per person

- Men eat meat pies almost twice as often as women

- 62 percent of meat pies are filled with chopped steak (ground beef)

- 36 percent are filled with steak and onion, steak and kidney, steak and potato, or steak and mushroom

- Just 2 percent are filled with chicken

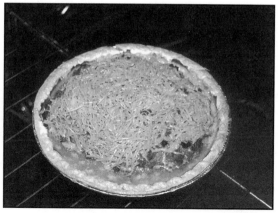

EPD Photos

*Meat pie, with dozens of recipe variations, is considered the Australian national dish.*

∞

## Australian Meat Pie

### Ingredients

2 pounds ground beef

1 cup ketchup

1 cup onion, chopped

1 teaspoon salt

1 cup milk

⅔ cup bread crumbs

1 teaspoon oregano

½ teaspoon pepper

2 Tablespoons Worcestershire sauce

2 cups cheddar cheese, shredded

2 prepared pie shells, 8-inch

### Procedure

1. Preheat oven to 350°F.

2. Combine ground beef, ketchup, onion, salt, milk, breadcrumbs, oregano, and pepper in a bowl.

3. Mix well.

4. Divide mixture into 2 pie shells and bake for about 45 minutes.

5. While the pies are baking, mix together Worcestershire sauce and cheese in another bowl.

6. After about 45 minutes, remove pies from oven.

7. Spread Worcestershire sauce and cheese mixture on top of pie shells.

8. Bake for about 10 more minutes, or until cheese is melted.

Serves 6.

∞

## Black Australian Coffee

### Ingredients

4 heaping Tablespoons decaffeinated coffee
    grounds

4 cups water

Pinch of salt

Pinch of dry powdered mustard (optional)

1 lemon, sliced crosswise into thin rounds

### Procedure

1. Measure water into a saucepan and heat.
2. Sprinkle coffee on top of water.
3. Add salt and mustard, if desired.
4. Heat the mixture slowly to the boiling point.
5. Remove from heat immediately.
6. Let stand for 5 minutes and strain.
7. Serve coffee with a slice of lemon in each cup.

EPD Photos

*Anzac biscuits have been popular with Australians for decades.*

∞

## ANZAC Biscuits

### Ingredients

1 cup margarine or butter

2 Tablespoons corn syrup

4 Tablespoons water

1 teaspoon baking soda

2 cups oatmeal

2 cups sugar

1 cup white flour

1 cup whole wheat flour

### Procedure

1. Preheat oven to 325°F.
2. Combine oatmeal, sugar, white flour, and whole-wheat flour in a bowl.
3. Melt margarine and add corn syrup and water in a small pan over heat.
4. Add the baking soda to pan and stir until fizzy.
5. Pour contents in pan into the bowl with dry ingredients and stir well.
6. Shape dough into balls and flatten with a fork on a tray.
7. Bake for about 15 minutes or until golden brown.

Makes about 4 dozen biscuits.

∞

## A Biscuit for a Treat?

Australians, like the English, call cookies "biscuits." They often use the nickname "bickies" or "bikkies" especially when offering a biscuit to a child (or even when offering a treat to a pet). Every household has a biscuit tin, a decorative round tin with a lid, to keep the supply of biscuits handy.

∞

## Lamingtons

### Ingredients

½ cup butter

1 teaspoon baking powder

¾ cup sugar

½ teaspoon baking soda

1 teaspoon vanilla extract

4 eggs

2 cups flour

½ cup milk

Pinch of salt

**For icing:**

4 cups confectioners' sugar

5 Tablespoons unsweetened cocoa powder

2 teaspoons butter

½ cup milk

Shredded coconut

### Procedure

1. Preheat oven to 350°F.

2. Mix together butter, sugar, vanilla, and eggs.

3. Slowly add baking powder, baking soda, flour, milk, and salt.

4. Pour mixture into an 8-inch square cake pan and bake for about 45 minutes.

5. Let cool and store overnight in a sealed container.

6. Make icing: Measure confectioners' sugar and cocoa into a large mixing bowl.

7. Heat milk and 2 teaspoons butter until the butter is melted. Add the milk gradually to the sugar mixture, stirring constantly. The icing should be fluid but not too runny.

8. Cut the cooled cake into 2-inch squares, and put the coconut into a shallow baking dish. Have ready a cooling rack set over a sheet of waxed paper to catch icing drips.

9. Holding a cake square with two forks, dip it into the icing, and then roll in the coconut. Transfer to rack to dry. Repeat until all cake square are coated.

Serves 16.

## 4 FOOD FOR RELIGIOUS AND HOLIDAY CELEBRATIONS

Most Australians spend holidays with family, participating in special events and preparing a festive meal. Since the temperatures are mild, meals are often consumed outdoors at a picnic or on the beach. Because Australia is in the Southern Hemisphere, the seasons are the opposite of those in North America and Europe. Christmas falls in the middle of summer, when most school children are on their summer vacation. A typical Christmas menu may include a variety of hot and cold meats, seafood, pasta, salads, and many types of desserts. Mince pies, fruitcake, shortbread, and plum pudding are also popular after-dinner treats.

Christmas puddings may contain a small favor baked inside. It is said that the person who finds the favor will be blessed with good luck.

Easter is also widely celebrated in Australia. A traditional menu consists of roast lamb, beef, or chicken with roasted vegetables such as potatoes, carrots, peas, or broccoli. Seafood, lasagna, and salads are also favorites. Pavlova, an elegant dessert made of egg whites and sugar and garnished with fruit, is a popular Easter dessert. Most children prefer candy, and chocolate eggs are Easter favorites. Treats are often shaped like an Easter bilby, an endangered Australian mammal that resembles the North American Easter bunny.

## Christmas Shortbread

### Ingredients

2 cups flour

1⅛ cups butter, cubed

⅓ cup sugar

2 Tablespoons rice flour (optional)

### Procedure

1. Preheat oven to 325°F.
2. Grease two cookie sheets.
3. Mix flour, sugar, and rice flour in a bowl.
4. Add the butter by rubbing in with fingertips.
5. Press mixture together to form a dough ball.
6. Place dough on a lightly floured surface.
7. Knead gently.
8. Divide dough in half, placing one rounded, ½-inch thick piece on each cookie sheet.
9. Gently mark out eight equal portions on each piece, radiating from the center.
10. Prick dough with a fork.
11. Bake for 30 to 35 minutes.
12. Allow the shortbread to cool and store in an airtight container.

## Pavlova

### Ingredients

4 egg whites

1 teaspoon cornstarch (corn flour)

Pinch of salt

1 teaspoon vinegar or lemon juice

½ teaspoon vanilla

¾ cup castor sugar (finer than regular sugar, but regular sugar may be substituted)

Whipping cream or whipped topping

Strawberries and kiwi for topping (other fruits or berries may be substituted)

### Procedure

1. Preheat oven to 250°F.
2. Cover a cookie sheet with cooking parchment.
3. In a very clean and dry bowl, use an electric mixer to beat egg whites until soft peaks form.
4. Slowly add sugar, sprinkling it into the bowl one spoonful at a time while continuing to beat the mixture until all the sugar has been added.
5. Sprinkle in the pinch of salt, and then slowly add the vinegar and vanilla, a few drops at a time. Finally, beat in the cornstarch.
6. Continue beating until the mixture stands in stiff peaks.

7. Place mixture onto the center of the paper on tray, and spread it into a circle about 8 or 9 inches in diameter (20 to 22 centimeters).

8. Make a slight indentation in the center.

9. Place the cookie sheet on the center rack in the oven and bake for 1 hour. Do not open the oven door while the pavlova is baking.

10. Leave pavlova in the oven to cool.

11. When completely cool, peel off the paper and place the pavlova on a serving plate.

12. Whip the heavy whipping cream with a teaspoon of sugar and ½ teaspoon vanilla.

13. Spread the pavlova with whipped cream and sliced fruit (kiwi and strawberries are traditional).

14. Slice and serve.

EPD Photos

*Mound spoonfuls of whipped topping into prepared meringue shells.*

∞

## Quick No-Cook Mini-Pavlova

While not authentic, this recipe will produce a dessert that resembles pavlova.

### Ingredients

6 meringue shells

Whipped topping

Strawberries and kiwi, sliced

EPD Photos

*Serve quick pavlova garnished with fruit such as sliced kiwi or strawberries.*

### Procedure

1. Place meringue shells on a serving tray.

2. Fill each with a generous dollop of whipped topping.

3. Cover with sliced strawberries and kiwi.

Serves 6.

## 5 MEALTIME CUSTOMS

Australians traditionally spent hours in the kitchen preparing meals for family and friends. The introduction of microwave cooking helped to speed the cooking process for busy Australian families, and also helped keep their kitchens cooler. As of 2000, nearly half of all households owned a microwave oven.

Australians eat three meals each day and enjoy an afternoon break for "tea and biscuits." Breakfast is normally eaten between

EPD Photos

*Chocolate Crackles combine crunchy rice cereal with a sweet chocolate coating.*

7 A.M. and 10 A.M. Lunch is increasingly being bought on the go as fast food. Australians' afternoon "tea and biscuits," served around 4 P.M., is usually composed of tea (or other beverage) accompanied by biscuits (cookies), small sandwiches, scones, or cakes. For school children, afternoon tea is the after-school snack. Dinner, the largest meal of the day, is served around 6 P.M. and is traditionally eaten European style, with the fork in the left hand and the tines pointing down, and the knife in the right.

Children normally enjoy snacks during the day, such as fruit, a beverage, or a small sandwich. Milo, similar to instant hot chocolate mix, is often used as an ingredient in snacks or drunk alone. Lamingtons, Chocolate Crackles (similar to crispy rice cereal treats in North America), ANZAC biscuits, or just a simple fruit salad, are also popular among children.

Restaurants offer a wide variety of cuisines for those who prefer to eat out. They often offer seafood and meats that are not normally prepared at home, such as stingray and emu (similar to the ostrich). Cafes offer lunch and afternoon tea and serve as meeting places. Such places also offer a variety of beverages. Coffee is growing in popularity, although tea is preferred in the afternoon and on Sundays, a traditional day for visiting with family and friends.

### Chocolate Crackles

**Ingredients**

4 cups crispy rice cereal

1 cup vegetable shortening or margarine

1 cup confectioners' sugar, sifted

3 Tablespoons cocoa

**Procedure**

1. Melt the shortening in a large saucepan over low heat or in a microwave oven.
2. Add crispy rice cereal, confectioners' sugar, and cocoa to the saucepan.
3. Spoon mixture into paper cupcake holders.
4. Chill for 12 to 24 hours in the refrigerator.

Makes 24 treats.

### Toast with Vegemite or Milo Spread

**Ingredients**

Toast

Vegemite (available at some supermarkets)

Milo spread

**MILO SPREAD**

½ cup butter or margarine

½ cup hot chocolate mix

**Procedure**

1. Toast 4 slices of bread.

EPD Photos

*Vegemite's distinctive jar with the red and yellow label may be found in large supermarkets around the world.*

2. Spread 2 slices with Vegemite spread.
3. Spread 2 slices with Milo spread.
4. Cut toast into triangles and serve with milk or juice as a snack. May be eaten as a light breakfast or after-school snack.

**MILO SPREAD**

1. To prepare Milo spread, combine butter or margarine and powdered hot chocolate mix in a bowl.
2. Beat the mixture until well combined.
3. Store the Milo mixture in a covered container in the refrigerator.

## 6 POLITICS, ECONOMICS, AND NUTRITION

Beginning in the 1980s, Australian adults (like adults in many developed countries) began to improve their eating habits, according to a 1995 Australian Bureau of Statistics study. Meat, a source of saturated fat, is being consumed less. Chicken and seafood are eaten more frequently. Fruits, vegetables, and grains are also consumed more often. There is, however, also an increase in the purchase and consumption outside of the home of foods and beverages that are generally higher in fat. Approximately 64 percent of men and nearly half of all women are overweight or obese.

The study included the diet of Australian children under the age of 15. It found that around one-third of children younger than 12 had no fruit in their diets, and more than one-fifth had no vegetables. The amount of sugar consumption, however, declined and vegetable consumption increased with age. The majority of children usually eat breakfast on five or more days per week, with 12- to 15-year-olds eating breakfast the least often.

Promoting healthy eating habits among children is an important issue in Australia. The government has allocated funding for community projects, mostly for the disadvantaged. Fresh and nutritious foods are often unavailable for children in rural and remote areas. Indigenous (native) groups, such as the Aborigines, frequently live in these disadvantaged areas.

## 7 FURTHER STUDY

### Books

Cook, Deanna. *The Kids' Multicultural Cookbook.* Vermont: Williamson Publishing, 1995.

Meisel, Jacqueline Drobis. *Australia: The Land Down Under (Exploring Cultures of the World).* New York: Benchmark Books, 1998.

Newman, Graeme and Betsy. *Good Food from Australia: A Down Under Cookbook.* New York: Hippocrene Books, Inc., 1997.

Pascoe, Elise. *Australia the Beautiful Cookbook.* San Francisco: Collins Publishers, 1995.

### Web Sites

Australia New Zealand Food Standards Council. [Online] Available http://www.anzfa.gov.au/ (accessed January 17, 2001).

The Australian Academy of Technological Sciences and Engineering. [Online] Available http://www.atse.org.au/ (accessed January 15, 2001).

The Australian Institute of Health and Welfare. [Online] Available http://www.aihw.gov.au/ (accessed January 17, 2001).

Australian Tourist Commission. [Online] Available http://www.aussie.net.au/ (accessed January 11, 2001).

BushLink: Inland Australia Online. [Online] Available http://www.bushlink.com.au/ (accessed January 17, 2001).

Concierge.com. [Online] Available http://www.concierge.com (accessed January 10, 2001).

Food Law and Policy Australia. [Online] Available http://www.ausfoodnews.com.au/ (accessed January 17, 2001).

Looksmart Australia. [Online] Available http://www.looksmart.com.au/ (accessed January 10, 2001).

Nutrition Australia. [Online] Available http://www.nutritionaustralia.org/ (accessed January 10, 2001).

Santa's Net. [Online] Available http://www.santas.net/australianchristmas.htm/ (accessed January 10, 2001).

# Australia
# Aborigines and Bush Tucker

## *Recipes*

Billy Tea ........................................................ 31

Damper (European style).............................. 32

Damper (Aborigine style) ............................ 32

Macadamia and Fruit Snack ........................ 33

Macadamia Nut Cookies .............................. 33

## 1 GEOGRAPHIC SETTING AND ENVIRONMENT

Aborigines (ah-bow-RIH-jeh-neez) are people who have lived in Australia for approximately 40,000 to 60,000 years. The word comes from the Latin words—*ab* and *origine*—which mean "from the beginning." Historically, the Aborigines were hunters and gatherers, and a small percentage were still living this traditional lifestyle as of the twenty-first century. Gathering plants or hunting animals usually depends on the climate. Central Australia is fairly dry and plants are sparsely scattered over the land. Aborigines rely on hunting animals and eating seeds and roots of plants for survival. In northeastern Australia, tropical trees offer a variety of fruits, vegetables, and nuts, including the popular macadamia nut. Those living along the coast who follow the traditional Aborigines lifestyle have access to seafood.

Most Aborigines are known to be skilled at growing things and most often use the land efficiently. Historically, they discovered that ashes from a fire acted as a natural fertilizer, providing nutrients for new plants to grow. Although this was successful, some groups living in the dry Australian desert regions often suffered a lack of food and were forced to move elsewhere.

## 2 HISTORY AND FOOD

Before the arrival of Europeans in the late 1700s, the Aborigines were successful hunters and gatherers. They lived off the land by understanding plants, animals, and natural resources. Aborigines continue to feel that they have a special relationship with the land.

The Europeans brought a new, unfamiliar way of life to the Aborigines. The European colonists established permanent

AUSTRALIA

0        500      1000 Miles

0    500   1000 Kilometers

hunt, and prepare traditional foods. As Europeans began to settle the territory of Australia, their cooking techniques and some imported ingredients were combined with the native foods favored by the Aborigines. For decades, the European settlers tried to convince—or force—the Aborigines to adopt the European way of life, especially in customs of food, housing, clothing, and education. The most drastic example of this is something the government did for approximately 150 years, ending in the early 1970s. The Australian government enacted programs to remove Aboriginal children from their homes and place them with families of European descent. The government hoped the Aboriginal children would replace their own traditional customs with the European customs of the majority population. But by the end of the twentieth century, the Australian government took action to recognize the Aboriginal way of life and to restore their property rights.

homes, prepared food in pots and pans, and traded goods outside of Australia. Some Europeans adopted customs from the Aborigines, such as food-gathering techniques, but most continued to live by European customs.

Along with a different way of life, the Europeans carried new diseases, often infecting the Aborigines, who had no resistance to foreign illnesses. Thousands of Aborigines died and their population decreased. Many who survived were forced to abandon their land and move to areas that were governed by the European settlers. This limited their ability to live a traditional lifestyle. It became difficult to grow, gather,

## 3 FOODS OF THE ABORIGINES

The Aborigines ate simple, balanced diets prior to the arrival of the Europeans in the late 1700s. Their diets contained meat and fish, as well as fruits, vegetables, and nuts. Honey was a popular sweetener, gathered from the hives of native bees found among the rocky crevices or in muddy riverbanks. Aborigines used many different ways to find the beehives. According to legend, an Aborigine hunter would catch a bee, and carefully attach something, such as a tiny fragment of a feather or a blade of grass, to it. This would help the tracker see the bee, and would also slow its flight slightly. The hunter would follow the bee back to its hive.

Native plants and animals the Aborigines ate became known as *bush tucker* (or *bush-foods*—bush is the term Australians use for natural territory or wilderness, and tucker is another name for food). Bushfoods—native and wild foods—became a national industry in Australia in the early 1980s. There were bushfood restaurants, growers, and packagers of the popular native Australian foods. This industry expanded well beyond the early bushfood industry—macadamia plantations—of the late 1800s.

*Bush tucker* varies depending on the region, climate, and season. Kangaroo, emu, and possum are available all year round and are popular meat choices among the Aborigines. Other meats, such as lizards, frogs, and turtles, are most often enjoyed during the summer. Seafood is also a common meal, particularly in communities along the seacoast. In the mountains of New South Wales, the Aborigines may feast on moths, which are rich in fat. The deserts of central Australia are home to witchety grubs (larvae) found in the roots of acacia bushes. The larvae, which are high in calories, protein, and fat, were once staples in the Aboriginal diet. Other insects in the traditional Aboriginal diet are bees, ants, and termites. Native edible plants include yams, onions, spinach, tomatoes, berries, and grass seed. Roots of some other native plants are also harvested to eat. Seeds and flowers of the acacia were ground to make a kind of flour that could be mixed with water to make a simple cake.

Probably the most widely recognized *bush tucker* recipe is *damper*, a simple type of bread made of water and flour. Although the Aborigines originally baked this bread,

it was the Europeans that gave it the name *damper*. Billy tea, named for the "billy" (pot) with a handle that is used for cooking over an open fire, is also popular. The billy is used to boil water for tea. Billy tea is now enjoyed by all Australians, both Aborigines and Europeans alike. When a sweet drink is desired, the water is sweetened with either honey or nectar collected from flowers. Some people also enjoy billy tea prepared according to the European custom of adding milk and sugar to the brewed tea, just before it is drunk.

## Billy Tea

### Ingredients

Billy pot (pot with handle, available at camping stores)

Water

Handful (2 or 3 Tablespoons) of loose tea leaves

Small fire (or stove burner)

Clean stick for stirring (wooden spoon or chopstick may be substituted)

Drinking mug

Sugar or honey (optional)

Milk (optional)

### Procedure

1. Fill billy pot ¾ full with water.

2. Place the pot on a burner and heat the water to a boil. (The traditional method is to hang the pot over an open fire.)

3. When the water is boiling, add the tea leaves.

4. Remove the pot from the fire or stove.

5. Stir leaves and water with stick (or wooden spoon).

6. Let the mixture stand (steep) for a few minutes, allowing the tea leaves to settle to the bottom of the pot. (Traditionally, someone would swing the pot by its handle in a wide circle over his or her head, using centrifugal force to settle the tea leaves. A safer method is to use the stick to tamp—push down—the leaves to the bottom of the pot.)

7. Pour the tea slowly into the drinking mug.

8. Add sugar (or honey) and milk if desired for taste.

∞

## Damper (European Style)

### Ingredients

2½ cups self-rising flour

1 teaspoon salt

1 teaspoon butter

1 teaspoon sugar

1 cup milk (or ½ cup powdered milk and 1 cup water)

### Procedure

1. Preheat oven to 350°F.

2. Grease and lightly flour a baking sheet.

3. Mix flour, salt, sugar, and butter together in a bowl.

4. Add milk and mix well. Knead the dough for about 5 minutes.

5. Shape into a flat circle and place on the baking sheet.

6. Bake for about 30 minutes. (Traditionally, balls of dough might be placed on rocks placed at the edge of a campfire to cook. Alternatively, wads of dough might be wrapped around the tip of a stick and held over an open fire to cook.)

EPD Photos

*To make Damper (European Style), shape dough into a large flat circle on a greased and floured baking sheet.*

∞

## Damper (Aboriginal Style)

### Ingredients

2 cups flour (not self-rising)

Pinch of salt

1 cup water (or enough to make a stiff dough)

### Procedure

1. Preheat oven to 350°F.
2. Mix flour and salt together. Add water slowly until a stiff dough is formed.
3. Pat the dough into a round shape on a greased baking sheet. Bake for one hour.
4. To serve, break off pieces. Discard crust if too hard, and eat the soft center. (Traditionally, the Aborigines would bake the dough in the ashes of the fire. The crust, dirty with ashes, would be torn away.)

### Macadamia and Fruit Snack

### Ingredients

1 jar macadamia nuts

1 package dried fruit (may be cranberries, raisins, cherries, or apples)

### Procedure

1. Combine nuts and dried fruit in a bowl.
2. To serve, shake a small amount from the bowl into the person's cupped hands, or use a cup or ladle to scoop servings out of the bowl.

## 4 FOOD FOR RELIGIOUS AND HOLIDAY CELEBRATIONS

Australia's national Journey of Healing Day, better known as Sorry Day, is probably the most significant modern national holiday for the Aborigines. In the 1970s, the government recognized that forcing the European lifestyle upon the Aboriginal people was wrong. It declared May 26 as "Journey of Healing Day" when all citizens celebrate Aboriginal culture and customs. The celebration includes parades, public speakers, and other festivities. Aborigines often use this day to show off some of their best native cuisine.

For Aborigines, food is closely associated with spirituality. They believe that everything living, including humans, was created by great spiritual beings. A key part of their spirituality is *Dreaming,* a belief that the great spirits live on in nature and through rituals. They believe that the spirits do not want them to eat certain foods. Customs of hunting, gathering, preparation, and cooking evolved through their religious beliefs. Each person feels a connection between himself or herself and a particular plant or animal. This special plant or animal is known as the person's *totem.* Many people do not kill or eat their totems, except during special ceremonies.

### Macadamia Nut Cookies

### Ingredients

½ cup butter or margarine

½ cup shortening

½ teaspoon baking soda

2½ cups powdered sugar

2½ cups flour

¼ teaspoon salt

2 eggs

1 cup macadamia nuts, chopped and roasted

*Macadamia nuts from native trees were gathered by the Aborigines when they lived solely in outlying areas of Australia.*

### Procedure

1. Preheat oven to 350°F.

2. Combine baking soda, powdered sugar, flour, and salt in a bowl.

3. In a separate bowl, mix the butter, shortening, and eggs until smooth.

4. Combine and mix together all ingredients into one bowl. Add nuts.

5. Drop teaspoons of dough about 2 inches apart on an ungreased cookie sheet.

6. Bake for 10 to 12 minutes.

Makes 3 to 4 dozen cookies.

## 5 MEALTIME CUSTOMS

Historically, Aboriginal males were responsible for hunting most animals, including birds, various seafood, and kangaroo. Larger animals, such as the kangaroo that is more challenging to catch, were often hunted by groups of hunters. Men used spears, harpoons, nets, traps, clubs, and even boomerangs for hunting wild creatures. Women tended to be responsible for the gathering of plants, shellfish, and insects. These gender roles continue today in traditional Aboriginal families.

Even when plants are plentiful, the Aborigines are careful not to waste. They use all parts of the plants, including seeds, roots, stems, leaves, and fruits. However, many plants require special preparation. Some are poisonous, others are tough, covered with prickly foliage, and most require washing, pounding, or grinding before they can be boiled in water.

Food preparation methods differ among regional groups, often depending upon climate. Food has often been cooked in the smoldering ashes remaining after a fire. Alternatively, food may be placed directly on top of glowing coals, boiled in water, or steamed in an oven-like pit in the ground. In the twentieth century, some Aborigines began to use modern products (such as aluminum foil) in traditional cooking techniques such as steaming. The billy (pot) introduced by Europeans is widely used by Aborigines to make cooking easier.

Historically, Aborigine children had to begin caring for themselves at an early age. Most were given their first small spear before age four or five. Sons would follow

∞

### Boomerang

The Aborigines use a type of boomerang that is different from the modern "returning boomerang" that is popular in modern-day Australia. When an Aborigine hunter throws a "non-returning boomerang," he uses a spinning motion. The boomerang hits the target with more force than a stick or rock. Many Aborigines also use the boomerang to scrape animal hides (and for other scraping tasks) and to start fires. Children use them as toys.

their fathers to watch how they hunted and made tools. Daughters would learn how to gather foods and prepare meals from their mothers. Some Aboriginal families continue to follow the occupations of their parents.

## 6 POLITICS, ECONOMICS, AND NUTRITION

At the beginning of the twenty-first century, nearly 400,000 Aborigines lived in Australia. Unfortunately, many of them are poor. Low incomes and living in isolated areas make it difficult for them to purchase food. Because of the cost to ship food to isolated areas, food sometimes costs almost twice as much in an outlying area than in densely populated urban regions. The long shipping distance may also cause fresh fruits and vegetables to spoil. As a result, rural community stores often carry convenience foods and pre-packaged processed foods. Such foods are often higher in fat, sugar, and salt. These foods may last longer on shelves, but sometimes lack nutrients that are needed for a healthy life.

With the majority of income being spent on purchasing food, less money is available for Aborigines to spend on utilities, such as electricity, gas and water for cooking, and refrigeration for storage. Convenience foods that do not require much preparation are favored over healthier foods. As a result, Aboriginal children and adults have a higher rate of health-related problems than other Australians. Poorer diets lead to a higher rate of obesity, diabetes, and heart disease.

## 7 FURTHER STUDY

### Books

Albyn, Carole Lisa and Lois Sinaiko Webb. *The Multicultural Cookbook for Students.* Phoenix: The Oryx Press, 1993.

Isaacs, Jennifer. *Bush Food: Aboriginal Food and Herbal Medicine.* Sydney, Aus.: Lansdowne Pub., 1996.

Kuper, Jessica. *The Anthropologists' Cookbook.* New York: Universe Books, 1977.

### Web Sites

Aboriginal Trail. [Online] Available http://155.187.10.12/anbg/aboriginal-trail.html (accessed January 19, 2001).

Australian Aborigines: History and Culture. Encyclopedia of Aboriginal Information A to Z. [Online] Available http://www.aaa.com.au/hrh/aboriginal/A_Z/atoz1.shtml (accessed April 6, 2001).

Australian Bureau of Statistics. [Online] Available http://www.abs.gov.au/ (accessed January 19, 2001).

Australia's Bushfood Industry. [Online] Available http://www2.dpi.qld.gov.au (accessed January 19, 2001).

BushTucker. [Online] Available http://www.arts.lunimelb.edu.au/amu/ucr/student/1997/silva/int_cooking.htm (accessed January 19, 2001).

Corroboree 2000: Towards Reconciliation. [Online] Available http://www.reconciliation.org.au/towards/pg3.htm (accessed January 19, 2001).

Food of the Australian Aborigines: 1000 BC–700 AD. [Online] Available http://library.thinkquest.org/C005446/text_version/English/aborigine.html (accessed January 19, 2001).

Price-Pottenger Nutrition Foundation. [Online] Available http://www.price-pottenger.org/Articles/Aborigines.html (accessed January 23, 2001).

Use of Insects by Australian Aborigines, Cultural Entomology Digest 1. [Online] Available http://www.bugbios.com/ced1/aust_abor.html (accessed January 19, 2001).

# Brazil

## Recipes

Ambrosia.................................................................. 38
Feijoada (Meat Stew) ............................................ 38
Orange Salad .......................................................... 39
Polenta (Fried Corn Mush) ...................................... 40
Pepper-Scented Rice ................................................ 41
Corn Cake................................................................ 41
Banana Frita (Fried Bananas) .................................. 42
Pudim (Thick Custard)............................................. 42
Pineapple-Orange Drink........................................... 43
Quejadinhas (Coconut and Cheese Snacks)................ 43

### 1 GEOGRAPHIC SETTING AND ENVIRONMENT

Brazil is the largest country in South America, and the fourth-largest country in the world. It lies on the East Coast of South America. Because Brazil lies in the Southern Hemisphere, the seasons are reversed from those in North America: the winter months are May through August, and the warmest summer month is January. The mighty Amazon River, the world's second-longest river after the Nile in Egypt, flows across northern Brazil. The area around the Amazon River is known as one of the world's largest rainforests. About one-fourth of all the world's known plants are found in Brazil. In the latter part of the 1900s, logging and other commercial industries were damaging the rainforest of Brazil. Dozens of animal and plant species became extinct in Brazil during the 1900s. The destruction of the rainforest environment has slowed a little, however. Brazil's soil is not fertile enough for agriculture in most areas, but it does produce large quantities of cocoa (it ranks third in cocoa production after Cote d'Ivoire and Ghana, both in Africa). River water that flows near cities is polluted by industrial waste.

### 2 HISTORY AND FOOD

Brazil is a large country that is made up of many different cultures. Each region has a different food specialty. The Portuguese arrived in Brazil in 1500 and brought their tastes and styles of cooking with them. They brought sugar, citrus fruits, and many sweets that are still used for desserts and holidays. The Brazilian "sweet tooth" was developed through the influence of the Europeans. Brazilians use many eggs, fruits, spices (such as cinnamon and cloves), and sugar to make sweet treats, such as ambrosia. They also use savory (not sweet) seasonings such as parsley and garlic. Other nationalities that settled in Brazil were Japanese, Arabs, and Germans. More than one million Italians had migrated to Brazil by 1880. Each immigrant group brought along its own style of cooking.

Long before the Europeans arrived, however, the Tupí-Guaraní and other Indian groups lived in Brazil. They planted *manioc* (a root vegetable like a potato) from which Brazilians learned to make tapioca and *farofa*, ground manioc, which is similar to fine breadcrumbs. It is toasted in oil and butter and sprinkled over rice, beans, meat, and fish. As of 2001, *farofa* was still used as the Brazilians' basic "flour" to make cookies, biscuits, and bread.

## Ambrosia

### Ingredients

4 cups milk

2 cups sugar

9 large egg yolks

1 Tablespoon lemon juice

4 whole cloves

### Procedure

1. Place the milk in a large saucepan and bring to a boil over medium-high heat.

2. Remove it from the heat, and add the sugar and the egg yolks, one at a time, mixing well with a wire whisk after each addition. Add the cloves and the lemon juice.

3. Cook over medium heat for about an hour, stirring occasionally, until the mixture becomes golden and grainy.

4. Chill and serve cold.

Serves 8.

## 3 FOODS OF THE BRAZILIANS

Rice, black beans, and manioc (a root vegetable like a potato) are the main foods for many Brazilians. The national dish is *feijoada*, a thick stew of black beans and pieces of pork and other meats. It is usually served with orange salad, white rice, *farofa* (ground manioc), and *couve* (kale), a dark green leafy vegetable that is diced and cooked until slightly crispy.

## Feijoada (Meat Stew)

### Ingredients

3 strips of raw bacon

2 onions

3 cloves garlic (or 1 teaspoon garlic powder)

1 pound smoked sausage

1 pound boneless beef (any cut of meat)

1 can (14-ounce) stewed tomatoes

1 cup hot water

1 Tablespoon yellow mustard

4 cups canned black beans

Salt and pepper

## Procedure

1. Cut the bacon strips into big pieces. Fry them in a large pot over medium-high heat for about 3 minutes, stirring often.

2. Turn the heat down to medium.

3. Cut the onion in half. Peel off the skin and outer layer. Chop both halves into small pieces.

4. Peel the cloves of garlic. Chop them into small pieces.

5. Add the onions and garlic to the bacon in the pot. Stir until the onions are soft, about 3 minutes.

6. Cut the sausage and beef into 1-inch pieces. Add them to the onions and garlic.

7. Cook until the meat is brown on all sides.

8. Add the stewed tomatoes (with juice), hot water, yellow mustard, and some salt and pepper. Turn the heat down to simmer. Cover the pot.

9. Cook for about 45 minutes, stirring often. If it looks too thick, add more water, ¼ cup at a time. Add the black beans (with liquid).

10. Cover the pot, and cook for 10 more minutes.

Serves 10 to 12.

EPD Photos

*This salad offers sweet, salty, spicy, and tart tastes in one dish. The fresh orange slices are sprinkled with salt, pepper, and sugar.*

❧

## Orange Salad

### Ingredients

5 oranges

1 teaspoon sugar

Salt and pepper

### Procedure

1. Peel the oranges and remove the inner core.

2. Cut the oranges into thin slices. Arrange the slices on a plate.

3. Sprinkle them with sugar, salt, and pepper.

4. Serve, or cover with plastic wrap and refrigerate until ready to eat.

Almost every kind of fruit grows in Brazil, including apples, oranges, peaches, strawberries, bananas, papayas, mangoes, and avocados. Fruits, vegetables, meat, and flowers are sold at *feiras* (street markets). These outside markets are set up on streets, which are closed to vehicle traffic. The markets are set up in a new location every day.

*Churrasco*, chunks of beef cooked on a metal skewer over hot coals, is another favorite. Sometimes the beef is soaked in a mixture of vinegar, lemon juice, and garlic before cooking. This "Brazilian barbecue" is served with rice, potato salad, *polenta* (fried corn mush), or, occasionally, a fried banana. *Gaúchos* (cowboys) living in the region of Rio Grande do Sul especially

EPD Photos

*Maté, an herbal tea-like beverage, is enjoyed in many parts of South America. The cup, made from a hollowed-out gourd, and metal bombilla (straw) are carried by gaúchos, hanging from their belts.*

enjoy *churrasco.* After the gaúchos eat their meal, they drink *maté* (an herbal tea drunk in many parts of South America). The tea leaves are placed inside a hollowed-out gourd, and then boiling water is poured over them. Gaúchos slowly sip the *maté* through a metal straw, called a *bombilla,* with a strainer on the lower tip of it. The gourd and straw are carried, hanging from the belt.

Another popular beverage is guaraná, made from a small red fruit that is high in caffeine and grows in the Amazon River area. It is a refreshing soft drink, unique to Brazil and with a taste some describe as similar to creme soda. People in the Amazon River area also chew the guaraná seeds, or make a drink by dissolving a powder made from the seeds in water. Powdered guaraná is available in the United States in some health food stores, or in markets specializing in foods from South America.

✎

## *Polenta (Fried Corn Mush)*

### Ingredients

3¼ cup water

¾ teaspoon salt

1 cup cornmeal

### Procedure

1. Stir ingredients in a saucepan over medium-high heat until they come to a slow boil.
2. Reduce heat to low, cover and cook for 15 minutes. Stir frequently.
3. Spread the polenta in a bread pan.
4. Wait until it is completely cool, then cut into 2-inch wide slices.
5. Fry them in a skillet over medium heat in 2 Tablespoons of butter, 10 minutes on each side until crunchy.

## 4 FOODS FOR RELIGIOUS AND HOLIDAY CELEBRATIONS

Although Brazil has no national religion, the Portuguese who arrived in Brazil in 1500 brought their Roman Catholic religion with them. About 75 percent of Brazilians consider themselves Roman Catholic. Those who do not follow the Roman Catholic religion still enjoy the world-renowned Brazilian Carnival tradition. During Carnival, colorful parades are held on the streets, and children and adults dress in costumes, dancing and celebrating in the streets all day and all night. People eat and drink continuously during Carnival, enjoying spice dishes, such as pepper-scented rice and feijoada, and sweets. Carnival is a week-long party that ends on Ash Wednesday, the beginning of the 40-day religious period of Lent before the Christian celebration of Easter. During Lent, it is a Roman Catholic tradition not to eat meat.

believe St. John protects the corn and green bean harvests, giving them plenty of food in the upcoming year. They celebrate St. John's Day with a harvest festival. Brazilians like to eat corn, as corn-on-the-cob and popcorn, and corn-based dishes such as corn puddings and corn cake, at all of the *Festivas Juninas*.

## Pepper-Scented Rice

### Ingredients

1 Tablespoon vegetable oil

1 small onion, finely diced

1 garlic clove, minced

1 cup long-grain rice

1 chili pepper

2 cups hot water

½ teaspoon of salt

### Procedure

1. Pour the vegetable oil into a large saucepan and heat for a few seconds. Add the onion, garlic, and rice.
2. Fry gently, stirring for about 4 minutes.
3. Add the chili pepper, hot water, and salt. Stir well and bring to a boil.
4. Simmer for 15 to 20 minutes, until the rice is soft and the water has been absorbed.
5. Remove the chili pepper and serve.

Serves 4.

*Festivas Juninas* (June Festivals) are held in honor of Roman Catholic saints—St. Anthony, St. Peter, and St. John. Brazilians

## Corn Cake

### Ingredients

1 can (11-ounce) corn, drained

7 Tablespoons softened butter

1 cup whole wheat flour

3 eggs, beaten

1 can (14-ounce) coconut milk

1 Tablespoon baking powder

2 cups granulated sugar

### Procedure

1. Preheat oven to 350°F.
2. Place all of the dry ingredients into a bowl and mix; slowly add milk, eggs, butter, and corn; mix until smooth.
3. Pour the mixture into a large greased loaf pan.
4. Bake for about 50 minutes.
5. To test if the cake is done, stick a toothpick into the center; the cake is done when the toothpick comes out clean.
6. Remove the cake from the pan by turning it over onto a wire rack to cool.
7. Slice and serve.

Serves 12.

Brazil is the world's largest producer of coffee, and Brazilians use coffee in many unique ways in cooking. For example, on Christmas Day, Brazilians prepare a turkey basted with a rich dark coffee with cream and sugar. The traditional stuffing contains *farofa* (ground manioc), pork sausage, onions, celery, and seasonings. Side dishes for this meal are mashed white sweet potatoes, *banana frita* (fried bananas), and green beans. Dessert is an assortment of fruit *doces* (sweetened fruits, preserved through slow cooking), star fruit, and strips of mango.

## Banana Frita (Fried Bananas)

### Ingredients

6 small bananas, peeled

1 large egg, beaten

1 cup fine bread crumbs

½ cup (1 stick) unsalted butter

Salt, to taste

### Procedure

1. In a mixing bowl, gently toss the bananas with egg to moisten, then lightly roll the bananas in the breadcrumbs.

2. In a large skillet, melt the butter over medium heat.

3. When the foam goes away, add the bananas and fry on all sides until golden.

4. Season with salt and serve hot.

Serve 6.

## 5 MEALTIME CUSTOMS

Because Brazil is the world's largest producer of coffee, a typical *pequeno almoço* (breakfast) consists of a cup of *café come leite* (a hot milk and coffee mixture) and a piece of French bread. Many Brazilian children also drink a coffee and milk mixture for breakfast.

Lunch, usually the biggest meal of the day, consists of rice, beans, salad, meat, or other dishes, depending on where the family lives and what they can afford to buy. Between lunch and supper some Brazilians have midmorning and midafternoon *café*, which includes coffee, hot milk, and cookies. *Pastels* and *empadas*, little pastries filled with any combination of shrimp, meats, and cheeses that are either fried or baked, are a favorite snack. These can be purchased by street vendors (Brazilian "fast food") or made at home.

In the late evening, many Brazilians eat a light supper. Children enjoy desserts such as *pudim* or *churros*, fried dough rolled in sugar and filled with caramel, chocolate, or sweetened condensed milk.

## Pudim
## (Thick Custard)

### Ingredients

1 pound sugar

½ tablespoon butter or margarine

½ cup water

6 egg yolks, beaten

1 cup shredded coconut

### Procedure

1. Preheat oven to 350°F.

2. Grease the cups of a 10 to 12 muffin tin and sprinkle with a bit of sugar.

3. In a saucepan, combine sugar and water. Bring to a boil, stirring until mixture forms a thin syrup.

4. Add butter and remove from heat and allow to cool.

5. When syrup is cool, add the egg yolks and coconut and mix well.

6. Pour mixture into sections of muffin tin.

7. Place tin in a larger pan filled with 1 inch of hot water.

8. Bake for 30 to 40 minutes.

9. To test if they are done, stick a toothpick into the center—it should come out clean.

10. When the custards are cool, turn the tin over onto a large platter.

Serve in bowls. Serves 12.

The Portuguese brought oranges and other citrus fruits to Brazil in 1500, and they are used in several dishes and juices. Students may enjoy a fruity drink, such as pineapple-orange drink, as an after-school snack.

EPD Photos

*Drop the coconut-cheese mixture by spoonful into baking cups.*

∞

## Pineapple-Orange Drink

### Ingredients

2 Tablespoons crushed ice

2 Tablespoons sparkling water or seltzer water

½ cup orange juice

½ cup pineapple juice

### Procedure

1. Pour the crushed ice and water into a large drinking glass.

2. Add the orange juice and the pineapple juice. Stir and drink.

This drink can also be made quickly in a blender. Serves 1 or 2.

Children may take *quejadinhas* (coconut and cheese snacks) to school as part of their lunch. These treats do not need to be heated and, if stored correctly, they stay fresh for several days.

∞

## Quejadinhas (Coconut and Cheese Snacks)

### Ingredients

1 cup tightly packed fresh grated coconut

1 can (8-ounce) sweetened condensed milk

2 Tablespoons freshly grated Parmesan cheese

2 large egg yolks

### Procedure

1. Preheat the oven to 450°F.

2. Place all of the ingredients in a medium-size bowl and mix well.

3. Place paper cups into the cups of a muffin tin. Drop the mixture by the spoonful into the paper cups.

EPD Photos

*Quejadinhas (coconut-cheese snacks) and orange-pineapple drink combine to make a delicious snack anytime.*

4. Place the muffin tin in a larger pan that has been filled with about 1 inch of water and cook for about 35 minutes.

5. These will keep well if they are stored in a tightly closed cookie tin.

## 6 POLITICS, ECONOMICS, AND NUTRITION

About 10 percent of the population of Brazil is classified as undernourished by the World Bank. This means they do not receive adequate nutrition in their diet. Of children under the age of five, about 6 percent are underweight, and over 10 percent are stunted (short for their age).

According to the Brazilian government, child poverty is one of the country's most serious concerns. About one-third of the children in Brazil live in poverty. Thousands of children spend their days on the streets of Brazil's cities; many abuse drugs and resort to crime and prostitution to get money to live. Many shopkeepers consider these street children a nuisance and ask police to keep the children away from their stores. International observers consider the child poverty in Brazil to be a human-rights issue, but many Brazilians see the children as a threat to security in the cities.

## 7 FURTHER STUDY

### Books

*Brazil*. Boston, MA: APA Publications, 1996.

Carpenter, Mark L. *Brazil, An Awakening Giant*. Parsippany, NJ: Dillon Press, 1998.

Ferro, Jennifer. *Brazilian Foods and Culture*. Vero Beach, FL: Rourke, 1999.

Harris, Jessica B. *Tasting Brazil: Regional Recipes and Reminiscences*. New York: Macmillan, 1992.

Idone, Christopher. *Brazil: A Cook's Tour*. New York: Clarkson N. Potter, 1995.

Serra, Mariana. *Brazil*. Austin, TX: Raintree Steck-Vaughn, 2000.

### Web Sites

LIMIAR. [Online] Available http://www.limiar.org/brazil/recipes (accessed February 22, 2001).

Recipe Xchange. [Online] Available http://www.recipexchange.com/recipexchange_cfmfiles/recipes.cfm/2660 (accessed February 26, 2001).

SOAR: Searchable Online Archive of Recipes. [Online] Available http://soar.berkeley.edu/recipes (accessed February 28, 2001).

# Brazil
# Afro-Brazilian

## *Recipes*

Quiabo (Okra)................................................ 46
Basic Rice ...................................................... 46
Moqueca (Spicy Fish and Coconut Milk Stew)............. 47
Moqueca aos Ovos (Spicy Egg Stew)......................... 47
Quindins (Coconut Macaroons) ................................ 48
Brazilian Black Beans ....................................... 49
Angu de Milho (Cornmeal Dish)............................... 49
Empadas (Little Baked Pies) ................................. 50
Acaçá (Steamed Rice Flour Pudding) ......................... 51
Olho de Sogra (Mother-in-Law Eyes).......................... 51

## 1 GEOGRAPHIC SETTING AND ENVIRONMENT

The majority of Afro-Brazilians live in the nine states of the country's northeastern section—home to nearly one-third of all Brazilians. Most Afro-Brazilians live near the coastal regions where there is an abundance of rainfall. The northeast states have three distinct areas. The flat coastal strip, which literally meals "forest zone," has rich soil that is suitable for the cultivation of sugarcane plantations. Vast hills and mountain ranges begin just miles from the fertile coastline. Highland shrubs and cacti grow here in large numbers. Lastly, the semi-arid interior covers nearly three-quarters of the northeast's area (however, the least amount of people live in this topographic region— mostly those of Portuguese or Indian descent). Soil quality is poor and rainfall is often unpredictable.

## 2 HISTORY AND FOOD

The Portuguese claimed the rights to the territory that makes up modern-day Brazil in 1500, and in 1532, they began bringing African slaves to Brazil. The Africans introduced the Brazilians to new cooking styles and tastes, such as cooking food in *dendê* (palm oil), using okra as a thickener and a vegetable, and using the banana in different dishes. Africans also introduced a wide variety of chili peppers and ginger to season food, and this practice has continued to be part of Brazilian cooking. Another cooking technique Africans took to Brazil was the use of dried smoked fish and shrimp. The oldest African dish in Brazil, *carurú*, dates back to the 1600s. It is a spicy stew made with smoked fish or shrimp, *quiabo* (okra), onions, *dendê* (palm oil), and peppers. In the twenty-first century, the African influence on ingredients and cooking techniques still thrives, especially in the northeastern state of Bahia.

## ∞
## Quiabo (Okra)

### Ingredients

2 cups water

1 pound small okra pods, topped and tailed

½ teaspoon butter

### Procedure

1. Place the water in a large saucepan and bring to a boil over medium heat.
2. Trim the tops and stem ends from the okra.
3. Place the okra in the water and cook for 3 to 5 minutes.
4. Remove from heat, drain, and serve hot with butter.

Serves 4.

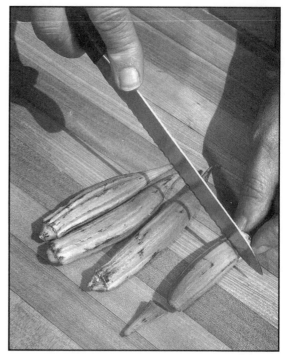

EPD Photos

*The tops and pointy tips (tails) of okra may be trimmed using clean scissors or a knife.*

## 3 FOODS OF THE AFRO-BRAZILIANS

Most of the descendents of the African slaves, who were brought to Brazil by the Portuguese in the 1500s, live in the state of Bahia. Although Afro-Brazilian cuisine can be seen throughout Brazil, it is especially noticed in Bahia, where the people have kept the culture, food, and *Candomblé* religion (a mix of Roman Catholic and African religions) alive. The Afro-Brazilian cuisine features *malagueta* (chili peppers), *dendê* (palm oil), seafood, coconut milk, banana, and okra.

*Vatapá* is one of the most popular Bahian dishes. It is a creamy dish served over rice, containing fish, shrimp, ground peanuts, coconut milk, *dendê*, and bread. Another favorite dish is *moqueca*, a stew made with fish, shrimp, crab, or a mixture of seafood in a *dendê* oil and coconut milk sauce. *Moqueca* is usually served over white rice.

## ∞
## Basic Rice

### Ingredients

3½ cups water

1½ cups long-grain rice

1 teaspoon salt

1 Tablespoon butter

**Procedure**

1. Bring the water to a boil in a saucepan over medium heat.

2. Stir in the rice, salt, and butter.

3. Cover and reduce the heat to low.

4. Simmer for about 20 minutes.

5. Remove the saucepan from the heat, and let it sit for about 5 minutes.

Serves 4 to 6.

## Moqueca
## (Spicy Fish and Coconut Milk Stew)

**Ingredients**

1 Tablespoon vegetable or olive oil

2 to 4 cloves garlic, peeled

1 onion, finely chopped

2 cups coconut milk

2 Tablespoons tomato paste

1 teaspoon fresh cilantro (remove stems), chopped

1 pound shrimp, shelled and deveined

2 Tablespoons white vinegar

2 limes

2 Tablespoons *dendê* oil (palm oil), optional

Salt

Pepper

Boiled white rice (prepared separately)

**Procedure**

1. Place the shrimp in a bowl. In a small bowl, combine the juice of one lime, vinegar, and salt. Pour over shrimp and set aside to marinate for at least 30 minutes.

2. Add 1 Tablespoon vegetable or olive oil to a large saucepan and heat over medium heat. Add garlic cloves and cook until golden brown.

3. Add onion and cook, stirring often with a wooden spoon, for about 5 minutes until the onions are softened.

4. Pour shrimp and marinade into pan.

5. Add cilantro, tomato paste, and pepper to taste.

6. Stir in coconut milk and bring the stew to a boil.

7. Lower heat and simmer 10 minutes until shrimp is cooked through.

8. Stir in *dendê* oil and cook for 5 minutes more. (This step may be omitted.)

9. Serve over boiled white rice.

Serves 6.

## Moqueca aos Ovos
## (Spicy Egg Stew)

**Ingredients**

12 eggs

3 Tablespoons olive oil

2 cloves garlic, minced

3 onions, thinly sliced

2 teaspoons fresh cilantro, minced

Salt and pepper, to taste

**Procedure**

1. Break the eggs into a bowl and beat gently.

2. Heat the oil in a large skillet over medium heat and cook the garlic, onion, and cilantro, stirring, until they are lightly browned.

3. Pour the eggs into the skillet, stir, and cook for a few seconds.

4. Reduce the heat to low, and continue to cook, stirring occasionally, about 5 minutes.

5. Season and serve hot over white rice.

Serves 4 to 6.

Afro-Brazilian cuisine is well known for its sweets and desserts, probably because of the influence of the Portuguese colonists who brought their love of sugar with them from their European homeland. The African slaves added their own style to the existing recipes. The women of the state of Bahia, the heart of Afro-Brazilian culture, make delicious sweets. One favorite is *cocada,* a coconut candy boiled in sugar water with ginger or lemon. *Quindins* (coconut macaroons) are another favorite sweet. *Quindins* are often served for dessert.

∞

## Quindins
## (Coconut Macaroons)

### Ingredients

¾ cup sugar

1 Tablespoon butter

1 cup tightly packed grated coconut

5 egg yolks

1 egg white, beaten into stiff peaks

### Procedure

1. Preheat the oven to 350°F.

2. In a medium-size bowl, mix the sugar, butter, and coconut together.

3. Beat in the egg yolks one at a time, stirring well.

4. In another bowl and using an electric mixer, beat the egg white until it is very stiff, and peaks remain on the surface when the beaters are lifted from the whites.

5. Fold (stir very carefully) the beaten egg white into the egg yolk mixture.

6. Grease the molds of a 12-muffin tin with butter and divide the mixture into the molds.

7. Place the muffin tin in a larger baking pan filled with 1 inch of water.

8. Bake for 35 minutes, or until the *quindins* are golden.

9. Let them cool and remove from the tin.

Serves 12.

## 4 FOOD FOR RELIGIOUS AND HOLIDAY CELEBRATIONS

The African slaves transported to Brazil by the Portuguese brought their religion with them. The religion of the modern-day Afro-Brazilians, *Candomblé,* is a blend of the

Roman Catholicism of the Portuguese, and African religions.

Throughout the year, people who follow *Candomblé* worship *orixás*, African gods and goddesses. *Orixás* are similar to Catholic saints. Each has a distinct name and a favorite food. People who follow the *Candomblé* religion eat meals made from the saint's favorite food on the day that saint is celebrated.

*Iemanjá*, the goddess of the ocean, is honored on February 2 of each year, and her favorite food is watermelon. Fishermen believe she protects them when they are out at sea, and that she will send large schools of fish for them to catch.

The god *Oxalá* (Jesus Christ), father of all *orixás,* is honored at the *Bonfim* festival, held each year on the third Thursday in January. Since black beans are thought to be *Oxalá*'s favorite food, many dishes for the festival are made with them.

## Brazilian Black Beans

### Ingredients

4 strips raw bacon

1 onion

2 cloves garlic

1 cup water

3 cans (14 ounces each) black beans

Salt and pepper

### Procedure

1. Cut the bacon strips into large pieces and fry them in a large pan over medium to high heat, stirring often.

2. Cut the onion in half and peel off the skin and outer layer. Chop both halves into large pieces.

3. Peel the cloves of garlic and chop into small pieces.

4. Add the onion and garlic to bacon, and cook until they are golden brown (about 3 minutes).

5. Add the water and black beans. Turn the heat to low. Cover and simmer for 20 minutes, until thick. If the beans look too thick, stir in more water, ¼ cup at a time.

Serves 6 to 8.

*Festivas Juninas* (June Festivals) are held in honor of certain *orixás* (the Catholic names for them are St. Anthony, St. Peter, and St. John). Corn, prepared in different ways, is eaten at all of the June Festivals, including puddings and cakes. One popular cornmeal dish, similar to polenta, is *angu de milho*.

## Angu de Milho (Cornmeal Dish)

### Ingredients

3 cups cold water

2 teaspoons salt

¾ cup cornmeal

4 teaspoons butter

### Procedure

1. Place half of the water (1½ cups) in a medium-size saucepan.

2. Add the salt, and bring to a boil over medium heat.

3. Slowly mix the cornmeal into the remaining 1½ cups water.

4. Gradually pour that cornmeal mixture into the boiling water, stirring constantly.

5. Add the butter and continue to stir continuously until it thickens where it can hold its shape.

6. Pour into a well-buttered 6-cup mold.

7. Let it cool before removing it from the mold.

Serves 4 to 6.

## 5 MEALTIME CUSTOMS

The heart of Afro-Brazilian culture, practiced by descendents of the African slaves brought to Brazil by the Portuguese, is in the state of Bahia in northeastern Brazil. A large percentage of the people living in these regions are poor. Afro-Brazilians usually eat foods that come from their surroundings, such as fruit and seafood. Other foods are bought at large produce markets in towns or from farms. Breakfast includes papayas, mangoes, pineapples, warm tapioca with milk and cinnamon, and coffee. Favorite snacks are *empadas* and *pastels*, little pastries filled with meat or fish and olives and cheese.

∞

## Empadas (Little Baked Pies)

### Ingredients

DOUGH:

2 cups flour

½ teaspoon salt

5 Tablespoons unsalted butter

1 egg

EGG WASH:

2 Tablespoons water

1 egg yolk

FILLING:

1 Tablespoon olive oil

1 onion, grated

1 tomato, peeled, seeded, and chopped

¼ cup canned chicken stock

⅛ teaspoon ground nutmeg

1 cup raw shrimp or cooked and shredded chicken

½ cup pitted green or black olives, chopped

1 Tablespoon parsley

Salt and pepper, to taste

### Procedure

DOUGH:

1. In a bowl, combine flour, salt, and butter.

2. Add the egg and 1 Tablespoon of the water and mix until smooth, and form into a large ball.

3. Cover and set aside.

EGG WASH:

1. Beat the egg yolk with the remaining 1 Tablespoon of water to brush the tops of the *empadas*.

2. Set the egg wash aside.

FILLING:

1. For the filling, heat the oil over medium heat in a medium skillet.

2. Add the onion and cook for 1 minute.

3. Add the tomato, stock, nutmeg, shrimp or chicken, olives, parsley, and salt and pepper.

4. Simmer and cook for 2 minutes.

5. Remove from the heat.

EMPADAS:

1. Preheat oven to 375°F.

2. On a lightly floured board, roll out the dough to ⅛-inch thickness. (Work with half the dough at a time if necessary.)

3. Using a large round cookie cutter or rim of a large glass, cut out circles in dough.

4. Place a heaping Tablespoon of the filling onto a circle of dough.

5. Fold in half and press the edges together with fingers or by pressing with the back of a fork.

6. Poke a hole in the top using a toothpick.

7. Brush the tops of the *empadas* with the egg wash, and place them on a baking sheet.

8. Bake for 20 minutes, or until golden brown.

Serves 6 to 8.

Along with other foods, street vendors (the equivalent to "fast food") sell the popular snack *acaçá* (steamed rice-flour pudding). It is prepared, wrapped in banana leaves, and steamed. In homes, *acaçá* is often eaten as a side dish with seafood meals.

∞

## Acaçá
### (Steamed Rice Flour Pudding)

**Ingredients**

2 Tablespoons olive oil

1⅓ cups canned unsweetened coconut milk

1 cup milk

1½ cups rice flour (available at Latin American and specialty food stores)

⅓ cup heavy cream

Salt and pepper, to taste

**Procedure**

1. In a large saucepan, mix together the olive oil, coconut milk, milk, and salt and pepper.

2. Bring to a boil over high heat.

3. Reduce the heat to medium and whisk in the rice flour a little at a time, stirring constantly until mixture is smooth and thick (about 8 minutes).

4. Gradually add the cream, mix, and pour into a lightly oiled 8x8-inch shallow oven-proof pan.

5. Let it cool for a few minutes.

6. Cut into small squares and serve.

Serves 8 to 12.

A popular dinner is *vatapá*, a creamy dish of fish, shrimp, ground peanuts, coconut milk, *dendê* oil, and bread, typically served over white rice. *Ximxim de galinha* (chicken with peanuts and cashews) is another well-known dish. Sorbet, or passion fruit-, mango-, lime-, or burnt coconut-flavored ice, is a favorite dessert. Another popular dessert, which has been made for many years, is *olho de sogra* (mother-in-law eyes). These are actually prunes stuffed with coconut, but they look like eyes.

∞

## Olho de Sogra
### (Mother-in-Law Eyes)

**Ingredients**

1 cup water

1¼ cup sugar

1 cup coconut, grated

2 large egg yolks

½ teaspoon vanilla extract

1 pound pitted prunes

Whole cloves, for garnish

**Procedure**

1. Place 1 cup each of the sugar, water, and coconut in a medium-size saucepan and cook over low heat until mixture thickens, about 15 minutes.

EPD Photos

*The sweet treats, Olho de Sogra (Mother-in-law Eyes), may be enjoyed anytime. Some people may prefer not to eat the whole clove in the center.*

2. Remove from heat and let cool.

3. Whip egg yolks until lemon-colored, and add them to the coconut mixture.

4. Add the vanilla and return mixture to stove.

5. Cook and stir over low heat for about 5 minutes.

6. Remove from heat and cool again.

7. Spread the prunes open lengthwise.

8. Stuff the inside of the prunes with the mixture.

9. Place a piece of clove in the center of the mixture.

10. Roll the prunes in the remaining sugar.

11. Serve them on a platter or in individual paper baking cups.

Serves 8 to 12.

## 6 POLITICS, ECONOMICS, AND NUTRITION

Living conditions for Afro-Brazilians are often dreadful, with an overwhelming number living in *favelas*, or slums. An estimated 69 percent of the population has no public sanitation, 63 percent does not have access to safe drinking water, and nearly 400,000 die of curable diseases each year due to poor health facilities. In addition, the Brazilian infant mortality rate, especially that of Brazilian children of African ancestry, is one of the highest in the world. Apparent discrimination of Afro-Brazilians has kept most uneducated, illiterate (unable to read), and living in poverty. Many Afro-Brazilians cannot afford the fresh and nutritious foods available to other Brazilians. According to the World Bank, those living in the impoverished areas of Brazil's northeastern states only make about one-tenth of the national average (approximately $230 each year).

## 7 FURTHER STUDY

### Books

Ferro, Jennifer. *Brazilian Foods and Culture*. Vero Beach, FL: Rourke Press, 1999.

Harris, Jessica B. *Tasting Brazil: Regional Recipes and Reminiscences*. New York: Macmillan, 1992.

Idone, Christopher. *Brazil: A Cook's Tour*. New York: Clarkson N. Potter, 1995.

### Web Sites

Department of Agricultural and Biological Engineering at Purdue University. [Online] Available http://pasture.ecn.purdue.edu/~agenhtml/agenmc/brazil/desserts.html (accessed February 27, 2001).

The Global Gourmet. [Online] Available http://www.globalgourmet.com/destinations/brazil/guarana.html (accessed March 14, 2001).

# Cameroon

## *Recipes*

Safou a la Sauce Tomate (Prunes in Tomato Sauce)..... 54

Easy Fufu...................................................................... 55

Traditional Fufu.......................................................... 56

Ndole (Bitterleaf Soup)............................................... 56

Banana and Pineapple Salad....................................... 58

Boiled Cassava ............................................................ 59

## 1 GEOGRAPHIC SETTING AND ENVIRONMENT

Situated in West Africa, Cameroon, shaped like an elongated triangle, contains an area of 475,440 square kilometers (183,568 square miles). Comparatively, the area occupied by Cameroon is slightly larger than the state of California.

There are four geographical regions: the western lowlands, which extend along the Gulf of Guinea coast; the northwestern highlands, which consist of forested volcanic mountains, including Mount Cameroon, the nation's only active volcano and the highest peak in West Africa; the central region, which extends eastward to the border with the Central African Republic; and the northern region, which is essentially a vast tropical plain that slopes down to the Chad Basin.

The southern and northern regions of the country are two distinct climatic areas. In the south there are two dry seasons, December to February, and July to September. The northern part of the country has a more comfortable climate.

## 2 HISTORY AND FOOD

Many staples of the Cameroonian diet came from the explorers of the New World (the Americas). The Portuguese arrived in Cameroon in 1472 and brought with them such foods as hot peppers, maize (corn), cassava (a root vegetable), and tomatoes.

Other Europeans settled on the Cameroon coast in the mid 1800s, with the British arriving first, followed by the French and Germans. The French influence is reflected in the presence of some foods, such as omelets and French bread, as well as in the preparation of some dishes; however, for the most part, Cameroonians continue to prepare their own traditional foods.

Foreign restaurants can be found in the larger towns and cities of Cameroon. In 2001, the city of Doula boasted a number of Parisian-style cafes, Greek, Lebanese, and Chinese restaurants, as well as places offering pizza and hamburgers. Restaurants in

EPD Photos

*Fried prunes are simmered in a savory tomato sauce and served over rice for a filling casual family dinner.*

the capital city, Yaounde, also offered a variety of cuisines, including Chinese, French, Italian, Russian, and traditional Cameroonian food. In the smaller cities, street vendors and restaurants serve more traditional favorites than foreign dishes.

∝

## Safou a la Sauce Tomate (Prunes in Tomato Sauce)

### Ingredients

12 prunes

1 cup water

2 cups tomato sauce

2 Tablespoons peanut oil

2 cups cooked rice

### Procedure

1. Rinse the prunes, cut them in half, and remove the pits.

2. In a saucepan, simmer the prunes with water until soft, about 4 minutes. Drain.

3. In a frying pan, heat the peanut oil over medium heat and fry the prunes, about 2 minutes.

4. Measure the tomato sauce into a medium saucepan, and add the fried prunes.

5. Cook over medium heat for 5 minutes. Serve over rice.

Serves 4 to 6.

# 3 FOODS OF THE CAMEROONIANS

The staple foods eaten by the people of Cameroon vary from region to region, depending on climate, and what is grown locally. In general, the Cameroonian diet is characterized by bland, starchy foods that are eaten with spicy (often very hot) sauces. Meat on skewers, fried and roasted fish, curries and peppery soups are common dishes.

Staple foods eaten in the north are corn, millet, and peanuts. In the south, people eat more root vegetables, such as yams and cassava, as well as plantains (similar to bananas). In both north and south regions, the starchy foods are cooked, then pounded with a pestle (a hand-held tool, usually wooden) until they form a sticky mass called *fufu* (or foofoo), which is then formed into balls and dipped into tasty sauces. The sauces are made of ingredients such as cassava leaves, okra, and tomatoes. The food most typical in the southern region of Cameroon is *ndole*, which is made of boiled, shredded bitterleaf (a type of green), peanuts, and melon seeds. It is seasoned with spices and hot oil, and can be cooked with fish or meat. *Bobolo*, made of fermented cassava shaped in a loaf, is popular in both the south and central regions.

Fresh fruit is plentiful in Cameroon. The native mangoes are especially enjoyed. Other fruits grown locally and sold in village marketplaces include oranges, papayas, bananas, pineapples, coconuts, grapefruit, and limes.

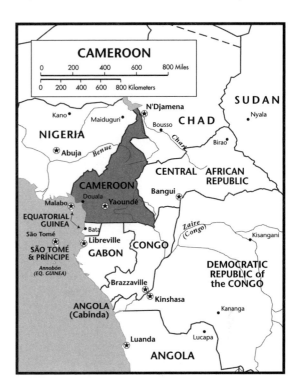

## Easy Fufu

*This is a good recipe to make with a friend, so you can share the job of stirring the stiff mixture and holding the pot steady. Neither the ingredients nor the process is authentic, but the results are similar in texture to the fufu prepared in Cameroon from cassava.*

### Ingredients

2½ cups instant flour mix (such as Jiffy Mix or Bisquick)

2½ cups instant mashed potato flakes

1 cup tapioca (made from cassava)

6 cups water

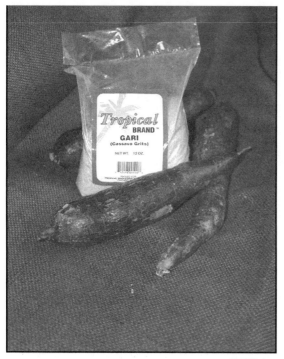

EPD Photos

*Cassavas resemble sweet potatoes, but have a shiny, brittle skin. Pictured with the cassavas here is a bag of gari (or cassava meal), which may be used to make fufu.*

### Procedure

1. Bring the water to a boil in a large pot.

2. Mix the instant flour mix, instant potato flakes, and tapioca together. Add the mixture to the boiling water, about 2 cups at a time. The mixture should be thicker and stiffer than mashed potatoes.

3. Stir constantly for 10 to 15 minutes while the mixture continues to boil. (The mixture will become very thick and difficult to stir, but it is important that it be stirred continuously.)

4. Let the mixture cool. Form the fufu into balls.

5. Serve with a spicy stew or soup.

Serves 8 to 10.

## Traditional Fufu

### Ingredients

2 to 4 pounds (4 to 8 large) white or yellow yams (not sweet potatoes)

### Procedure

1. Scrub the yams. Place them in a large pot and cover them with water.

2. Bring the water to a boil and cook for 20 to 30 minutes, until the yams are soft. (The skins will be easy to cut through with a fork or knife.)

3. Drain yams into a colander, and run cold water over them to cool them.

4. Remove peels from yams and return them to the pot.

5. Using a potato masher or wooden spoon, mash and beat the yams for 10 to 15 minutes until completely smooth. (A helper can hold the pot steady while the yams are being beaten.)

6. Shape the fufu into balls and serve with stew, sauce, or gravy.

Serves 8 to 10.

## Ndole (Bitterleaf Soup)

### Ingredients

2 cups dried bitterleaf (can substitute spinach, kale, collards, or turnip greens)

½ pound cooked shrimp (or one cup dried shrimp, if available)

1 cup natural-style peanut butter

1 large onion, chopped

2 cups water

2 Tablespoons fresh ginger, grated

2 cloves garlic, crushed

6 tomatoes, chopped

*Fruits available in village markets include (left to right) bananas, papaya, mango (front), coconut (back), oranges (front), and limes.*

2 to 3 Tablespoons vegetable oil

Salt and pepper, to taste

**Procedure**

1. (If using any greens other than bitterleaf, skip this step.) Soak the bitterleaf overnight; drain in the morning and press out the excess water.

2. If using kale, collards, or turnip greens, wash the greens, chop them, and cook them in a pot of boiling water for 5 minutes.

3. If using spinach, wash the leaves and chop the spinach.

4. Heat 2 Tablespoons of oil in a large pot and add the onions, garlic, and ginger. Sauté for 3 minutes.

5. Add the chopped tomatoes, reduce heat, and simmer for about 3 minutes.

6. Add the greens and simmer, stirring frequently, about 5 minutes.

7. Add the peanut butter. Stir to combine well, cover the pot, and continue simmering until greens are tender (about 15 minutes). If mixture seems too dry, add water, ½ cup at a time.

8. Cut shrimp into small pieces.

9. Cook for 10 more minutes, then add the spinach.

10. Serve with rice or boiled plantains and fufu.

Serves 6 to 8.

## 4 FOOD FOR RELIGIOUS AND HOLIDAY CELEBRATIONS

During the month long observance of the holiday of Ramadan, Cameroon's Muslims fast from dawn to dusk. This means they are forbidden to eat or drink during this time. The evening meal during Ramadan may include a rich soup. In most areas, a *fete des mouton* festival is celebrated two months after Ramadan to remember the willingness of Abraham to sacrifice a sheep from his flock. This celebration lasts for several days, during which it is customary for people to slaughter a sheep and then visit their friends and neighbors, giving them gifts of meat.

Most Cameroonians celebrate Christmas, even those who are not Christian. It is a time for visiting friends and family, and exchanging gifts. Holidays and events, such as coronations; saying goodbye to someone going abroad; weddings, and even funerals, are marked by feasts and meals at which friends and neighbors gather to eat local favorite dishes. It is traditional to slaughter and cook a sheep or goat at important occasions. Chicken dishes are also popular holiday fare.

∞

### Banana and Pineapple Salad

**Ingredients**

2 firm ripe bananas, peeled and sliced

2 firm ripe tomatoes, sliced

1 small pineapple, peeled and sliced

1 avocado, peeled, pitted, and sliced

1 Tablespoon roasted peanuts, chopped

1 can coconut milk

**Procedure**

1. Boil the coconut milk until it thickens.
2. Set it aside to cool.
3. Pile the bananas, tomatoes, pineapple, and avocado alternately in layers in individual glass dishes.
4. Top with chopped peanuts and the thickened coconut milk.
5. Serve cold.

Serves 4 to 6.

## 5 MEALTIME CUSTOMS

At mealtime, damp towels may be passed out to diners (before and after the meal), to wash their hands; Cameroonians eat out of communal bowls. Using their right hands, they dip three fingers into the starchy food—often *fufu* or a millet dish—and then into the stews or sauces of the meal. It is customary for the men to serve themselves first, while the women wait patiently and the children eat what is left after the adults have finished.

People of Cameroon eat three meals a day. A variety of foods, including fruit, porridge, and boiled plantains, may be eaten for breakfast. Eggs and boiled cassava are also popular choices. Lunch and dinner are likely to feature a starchy dish such as *fufu*, boiled cassava, rice or millet, generally served with a vegetable soup or a hearty stew.

Meal preparation is very time consuming. Preparation of *fufu*, for example, can take days. The cassava or yams must be boiled and pounded into a pulpy mass. The preparation of *fufu* from powdered starch or rice is less complicated, but still requires much stirring. Cooking in the villages generally takes place over wood or charcoal fires, with iron pots and wooden spoons. In towns, canisters of propane may be used to power gas stoves. Even at the beginning of the twenty-first century electricity is seldom available for cooking use except in the largest cities.

## ∞
## Boiled Cassava

**Ingredients**

2 cassava

Water

1 teaspoon salt

**Procedure**

1. Wash the cassava, then peel off the thin white and brown skins.
2. Cut the cassava into 3- to 4-inch long pieces.
3. Cut each piece in two and remove the midrib.
4. Place the cassava into a pot with enough water to cover the cassava half way. Add salt.
5. Boil until the cassava is soft, but not falling apart.
6. Drain and serve hot with fish or meat stew.

Serves 2 to 4.

## 6 POLITICS, ECONOMICS, AND NUTRITION

The government has tried for years to improve nutrition and health care, but there is a shortage of doctors and medical supplies, so the life expectancy is just about fifty years. Less than half the children receive immunization against common diseases such as tuberculosis, polio, and measles.

Families spend about one-third of their income on food—mostly on plantains, cassava, corn, millet, and small amounts of meat. Peanuts, called groundnuts, are an important source of protein.

## 7 FURTHER STUDY

### Books

Cusick, Heidi Haughy. *Soul and Spice*. San Francisco: Chronicle Books, 1995.

Hudgens, Jim and Richard Trillo. *The Rough Guide to West Africa*. London: Rough Guides, Ltd., 1999.

Iodowu, K. E. *Auntie Kate's Cookery Book*. Cameroon: published privately, 1976.

### Web Sites

California Academy of Sciences, Traditional Arts Program. [Online] Available http://www.calacademy.org/research/anthropology/tap/archive/1999-10--soya.html (accessed April 11, 2001).

CARE. [Online] Available http://www.care.org/info_center/field_notes/cameroonft.html (accessed April 11, 2001).

U.S. Peace Corps. [Online] Available http://www.peacecorps.gov/wws/water/africa/countries/cameroon/dailyusage.html (accessed April 11, 2001).

University of California, Berkeley, Searchable Online Archive of Recipes. [Online] Available http://soar.Berkeley.EDU/recipes/ethnic/africa/indexall.html (accessed April 11, 2001).

Welcome to Cameroon. [Online] Available http://www.telp.com/cameroon/index.htm (accessed April 11, 2001).

Weekend Special, Le Magazine de Afric'Netpress. [Online] Available http://www.iccnet.cm/cam_actu/samdim/damez.htm (accessed April 16, 2001).

### Sources for Special Ingredients

African Food Club [Online] Available http://www.africanfoodclub.com (accessed April 19, 2001).

Cassava, plantain, and other ingredients can be found in the produce section of larger grocery stores, as well as in Asian and African specialty stores in many areas of the United States.

# Canada

## *Recipes*

Sauteed Fiddleheads ..................................... 63
Canadian Bacon with Maple Glaze ............................. 63
Sweet Corn Pancakes ..................................... 64
Canada Day Cake........................................ 65
Nanaimo Bars ........................................ 65
Maple Sundae......................................... 67
Fish and Brewis ....................................... 67
Maple Syrup Upside-Down Cake................................ 67

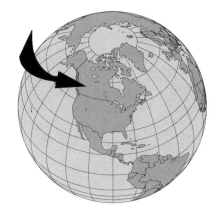

### 1 GEOGRAPHIC SETTING AND ENVIRONMENT

Canada is the world's second-largest country (after Russia), and is the largest country in North America. The eastern provinces, known as the Maritimes, are separated from the rest of the country by low mountain ranges. Newfoundland and Prince Edward Island are island provinces in the Atlantic Ocean.

Along the border with the United States in the center of Canada is a fertile plain bounded by the Saint Lawrence River, Lake Ontario, and the Hudson Bay. Also along the U.S. border further to the west are farms and ranches. Extending through western Alberta to the Pacific Ocean is the northern portion of the Rocky Mountain range. Mount Logan, at 19,524 feet (5,915 meters) the highest peak in Canada, is near the Alaska border. The climate varies across the vast Canadian territory. The west coast gets about 60–120 inches (150–300 centimeters) of rain each year; the center part of the country gets less that 20 inches (50 centimeters), and the Maritime provinces 45–60 inches (115–150 centimeters). In British Columbia, there are 252 rainy days each year, but in the center of the country, there are just 100.

### 2 HISTORY AND FOOD

France and England battled over who would colonize the territory of Canada in the late 1400s. The English explorer John Cabot arrived in Newfoundland in 1497. About 40 years later in 1534, Jacques Cartier began his exploration of Canada on behalf of France. By the early 1600s, there were permanent French colonies, and in 1663, New France was established as a territory of France. French fur traders competed with the traders of the Hudson's Bay Company, run by British merchants. Wars in North America, known as the French and Indian wars, were waged in the 1700s. The Treaty of Paris in 1763 ended the armed fighting and established British rule over all of the territory formerly called New France.

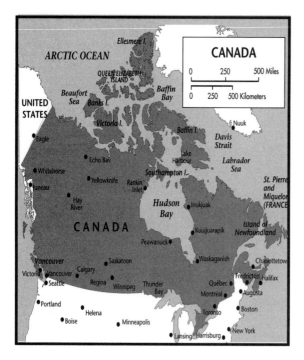

States, made simple, hearty meals from available ingredients. In northern Canada—Northwest, Yukon, and Nunavut territories—the diet is limited by the short growing season, dominated by preserved food ingredients, and influenced by the native Inuit diet. And along the west coast in British Columbia, immigrants from Asian nations influence food and cultural practices. In Vancouver in the west and Toronto in the east (and in many places elsewhere in Canada), Lunar New Year celebrations were inspired by the citizens of Asian heritage living there, but are enjoyed by many other Canadians as well.

## 3 FOODS OF THE CANADIANS

The favorite foods of Canadians vary slightly from region to region, and are strongly influenced by their family heritage, especially in relation to holiday celebrations. Along the Atlantic coast, seafood and dishes derived from English traditions (except in Quebec) are common. In Quebec, favorite foods come from the area's French heritage. Throughout Canada, maple syrup and maple products are popular, reflecting the significance of the maple tree, whose leaf adorns the flag of Canada. Many families enjoy a visit in early spring to a maple sugar "shack," the special rustic building where sap from maple trees is boiled in a large open pan to make maple syrup.

Later in the spring, many people in Eastern Canada visit a wooded area to harvest fiddleheads. Fiddleheads, named because they look like the coiled end of a violin ("fiddle"), are the tasty new sprouts of woodland ferns, picked before they develop into large lacy fronds. They are a fragile

In 1846 conflict over the western portion of the United States–Canada border was resolved, and the border was set at 49°north latitude. This border has been undisputed every since.

Food and other customs in Canada still carry hints of the colonial influences of England and France. Canadians speak English except in Quebec, where the language is French, reflecting the influence of French settlers. But there are other regional differences in food and customs, too.

Food in the provinces of Eastern Canada shows signs of English heritage, except in Quebec where the influence is French. In the provinces of Western Canada, the cuisine reflects the explorers and settlers, who, like their southern neighbors in the United

spring specialty, usually available for just a few weeks in the spring. Grocery stores in Canada may stock frozen fiddleheads alongside other frozen vegetables.

## ∞
## Sauteed Fiddleheads

### Ingredients

1 bunch fiddleheads

1 Tablespoon butter

1 Tablespoon olive oil

### Procedure

1. Trim the fiddleheads so that the stem end is about 2 inches long. Rub the dry brown flakes off the fiddleheads, and rinse well.

2. Fill a saucepan with cool water and plunge the fiddleheads into the water to rinse off any grit.

3. Remove the fiddleheads from the pan, change the water, and repeat the soaking. Rinse the fiddleheads under running water to remove any remaining grit.

4. Rinse and dry the saucepan. Measure oil and butter into it and heat until the butter is melted.

5. Add the fiddleheads and sauté, stirring with a wooden spoon, for about 5 minutes. Fiddleheads will be bright green and crispy.

Serves 8 to 10.

## ∞
## Canadian Bacon with Maple Glaze

### Ingredients

½ cup cider vinegar

¾ cups maple syrup

1 Tablespoon brown sugar

1 pound (approximately) Canadian bacon

### Procedure

1. Preheat oven to 300°F (150°C).

2. Combine vinegar, maple syrup, and brown sugar in a bowl. Set aside.

3. Slice Canadian bacon about ½-inch thick. Arrange the slices in a casserole or baking dish, and spoon the syrup mixture over the slices.

4. Bake for 30 minutes. Serve hot or at room temperature. (To serve as a snack, cut slices into bite-sized pieces and serve with toothpicks.)

Serves 6 for lunch or dinner, or 15 to 20 as a snack.

Western Canadians enjoy the products of the large ranches and farms in that part of the country. Barbecued food, beef, and corn dishes, such as Sweet Corn Pancakes, are popular. Berries such as blueberries and saskatoon berries, are popular accompaniments to pancakes, waffles, and are often made into syrups, jams and preserves.

## ❧
## *Sweet Corn Pancakes*

### Ingredients

6 eggs, separated (Note: to separate eggs, crack the egg and allow just the white to fall into a bowl, holding the yolk in one of the shell halves. Transfer the yolk back and forth between the two shell halves, being careful not to break it, until all the white has dripped into the bowl. Put the yolk into a separate bowl.)

¼ cup half-and-half

1 Tablespoon sour cream

⅓ cup flour

1 teaspoon baking soda

1 teaspoon baking powder

½ cup corn (may be fresh or frozen corn kernels)

Vegetable oil to oil the pan

### Procedure

1. Beat the egg whites until they hold soft peaks when the beaters are lifted up.

2. In another bowl, combine the egg yolks, half-and-half, and sour cream.

3. Gradually add the dry ingredients to the egg yolk mixture. Add the beaten egg whites, using a gentle stirring motion to combine them with the yolk mixture.

4. Add the corn, and stir gently. Pour a small amount of oil into a non-stick pan and heat it over medium heat. Drop batter, about 1 Tablespoonful at a time, into the pan for each pancake and cook until golden brown on each side.

Serves 4 to 6.

While Canada is known to some for its beers (such as Molson and Labatts), nonalcoholic beverages that are favorites in Canada are spruce beer (made from spruce trees, a specialty of eastern Canada), and apple and cherry ciders.

## 4 FOOD FOR RELIGIOUS AND HOLIDAY CELEBRATIONS

Canadian Thanksgiving is celebrated on the second Monday in October. A typical menu for Thanksgiving is similar to that served in the country's neighbor to the south, the United States.

Burns Day is celebrated January 25 to commemorate the birthday of poet Robert Burns (1759–96). It is especially significant for people of Scottish descent worldwide, and Scots Canadians are no exception. On Burns Day, the menu includes such Scottish favorites as haggis, cockaleekie soup (chicken-based leek soup), and Dundee cake (a rich fruitcake).

---

## ❧
## *Thanksgiving*

Beet Soup

Roast Turkey with Corn Bread Stuffing

Cranapple Relish

Brussels Sprouts

Mashed Potatoes

Burnished Squash Wedges

Pumpkin Pie

---

## ∞
## *Canada Day Cake*

### Ingredients

1 white or yellow cake mix

1 container white frosting

1 quart strawberries

Picture of flag of Canada

### Procedure

1. Prepare cake according to package directions. Bake in a 9-inch by 13-inch cake pan. Allow cake to cool.

2. Frost cake with white frosting. Using a knife or spatula, make surface of frosting as smooth as possible. (It may help to dip the knife or spatula into a glass of water.

3. Slice the strawberries, and arrange in rows at the left and right edges of the cake to represent the stripes at the edges of Canada's Maple Leaf Flag.

4. Referring to the picture of the flag, arrange the slices strawberries in the center of the cake to represent the Maple Leaf.

Serves 24.

On Canada Day (July 1), Canadians celebrate with picnics and fireworks (similar to the Fourth of July in the United States). Dishes served are typical casual dining fare, such as hamburgers, hot dogs, and table settings feature the patriotic color scheme of Canada's red and white maple leaf flag.

A common treat served across Canada is the nanaimo bar. It is believed that nanaimo bars, a sweet bar cookie made in layers, originated in the 1950s in the Vancouver area, when a recipe was published in the

EPD Photos

*A sheet cake, decorated with strawberries to represent Canada's Maple Leaf flag design, is a fitting dessert for a Canada Day celebration.*

*Vancouver Sun* newspaper. Since then, many variations on the original recipe have been developed. The recipe appears more complicated than it is because of the three separate layers.

## ∞
## *Nanaimo Bars*

*Nanaimo Bars have three layers.*

### Ingredients for bottom layer

½ cup butter

¼ cup sugar

⅓ cup unsweetened cocoa

1 egg

1 teaspoon vanilla

2 cups crushed graham crackers (packaged graham cracker crumbs may be used)

1 cup shredded coconut

½ cup chopped walnuts

### Ingredients for middle layer

¼ cup butter

2 cups confectioners' sugar

2 Tablespoons vanilla custard powder (available in Canada, but not in the United States; instant vanilla pudding powder may be substituted)

3 Tablespoons milk

### Ingredients for top layer

4 ounces semi-sweet chocolate

1 Tablespoon butter

### Procedure

1. *Make bottom layer:* Grease a 9-inch square cake pan.

2. Combine ½ cup butter, sugar, cocoa, egg, and vanilla in a heavy sauce pan. Heat over low heat, stirring constantly, until mixture thickens.

3. Add graham crackers crumbs, coconut, and chopped walnuts, stirring to combine. Press the mixture in the greased pan.

4. *Make middle layer:* Beat together ¼ cup butter, confectioners' sugar, vanilla custard or pudding powder, and milk, until the mixture is creamy.

5. Spread over graham cracker base in cake pan. Refrigerate bars until firm, at least 1 hour.

6. *Make topping:* Melt semi-sweet chocolate and 1 Tablespoon butter. Drizzle over chilled bars. Return to refrigerator to chill until firm (at least 1 hour).

7. Cut into squares and serve.

Serves 16.

## 5 MEALTIME CUSTOMS

Most Canadians eat three meals each day, with breakfast featuring cold cereal, pastries, fruit juices, and hot beverages such as

EPD Photos

*Hard Bread, not widely available in the United States, is rock-like and dry before soaking overnight in water.*

coffee, tea, or hot chocolate. At around noon, Canadians may enjoy a sandwich or soup; students may carry a ham and cheese sandwich, chips or pretzels, and fruit to eat a noon during the school lunch break.

For dinner, depending on where they live, Canadians may have seafood (west coast or Maritime east coast provinces), beef (western Canada, especially Alberta), or chicken or pork. Many Canadians enjoy gravy, serving it frequently with potatoes prepared in many different ways. A traditional Newfoundland dish, Fish and Brewis, features ingredients that may be stored through the long winter months. Desserts featuring maple syrup, such as Maple Syrup Upside-Down Cake or a simple Maple Sundae, are popular treats.

∞

## Maple Sundae

### Ingredients

3 Tablespoons pure maple syrup

Vanilla ice cream

Chopped nuts (optional)

Whipped topping (optional)

### Procedure

1. Spoon vanilla ice cream into bowls.

2. Drizzle about 3 Tablespoons of maple syrup over the ice cream.

3. Top with chopped nuts and whipped topping (if desired), and serve immediately.

Serves 1.

∞

## Fish and Brewis

2 pounds salt cod

6 loaves Hard Bread (not readily available in the United States; see Source of Special Ingredients)

1 cup salt pork

### Procedure

1. Place salt cod in a saucepan, cover with water, and allow to soak overnight. Place Hard Bread in another saucepan, cover with water, and allow this to soak overnight also.

2. *Make fish:* Drain salt cod and return to saucepan. Refill saucepan with fresh water, heat to simmering, and cook, covered, for 20 minutes. Drain, flake the fish into serving-sized pieces, and arrange with Hard Bread (called *brewis*) on a serving platter.

3. *Make brewis (Hard Bread):* Do not drain Hard Bread. Heat over medium-low heat until water simmers. Simmer, covered, for about 15 minutes. Drain and place cooked Hard Bread, known as *brewis*, on a serving platter with fish. Place the platter, loosely covered, in the oven on the lowest setting to keep warm.

4. *Make scrunchions:* Dice the salt pork into small cubes and sauté them in a skillet until golden brown.

5. Serve the fish and brewis, topped with scrunchions.

Serves 6 to 8.

∞

## Maple Syrup Upside-Down Cake

### Ingredients

1 cup maple syrup

1 Tablespoon butter, softened

3 Tablespoons sugar

1 egg

1 cup flour

2 teaspoons baking powder

Pinch of salt

¼ teaspoon cinnamon or nutmeg

½ cup milk

¼ cup chopped walnuts (optional)

Vanilla ice cream or whipped topping as accompaniment (optional)

## Procedure

1. Preheat oven to 350°F (175°C)

2. Measure butter, sugar, and egg into a bowl, and beat with a wooden spoon or electric mixer until creamy.

3. Mix flour, baking powder, salt, and cinnamon (or nutmeg) together. Add the dry ingredients and the milk, a little at a time and alternating between the two, to the creamed butter mixture. Stir until well blended.

4. Measure syrup into a small saucepan. Heat the syrup until it boils, and pour into a generously buttered 8-inch square baking pan. If using chopped walnuts, add them to the hot syrup.

5. Scoop up the dough in four large balls and drop them into the hot maple syrup. Using two forks, stretch dough the edges of the balls until the dough forms one large mass. Bake at 350°F (175°C) for 30 minutes.

6. Serve warm, with ice cream or whipping cream (if desired).

Serves 16.

## 6 POLITICS, ECONOMICS, AND NUTRITION

Only about 5 percent of Canada's land is considered arable (able to grow crops), and agriculture contributes about 2 percent to the country's gross domestic product. The trend is toward larger farms. Canadian farms produce grains such as wheat, barley, corn, and oats. Canada ranks third in the world in grain exports. Canadian farmers and ranchers also raise livestock for export, especially in Alberta, Saskatchewan, and Manitoba.

## 7 FURTHER STUDY

### Books

Barbolet, Herb. *Farm Folk, City Folk: Stories, Tips, and Recipes Celebrating Local Food for Food Lovers of All Stripes.* Vancouver: Douglas & McIntyre, 1998.

Barer-Stein, Thelma. *You Eat What You Are: People, Culture, and Food Traditions.* 2nd ed. Toronto, Ont.: Firefly Books, 1999.

Chavich, Cinda. *The Wild West Cookbook.* Don Mills, Ont.: R. Rose, 1998.

Claman, Marcy. *Rise & Dine Canada: Savory Secrets from Canada's Bed & Breakfast Inns.* 2nd ed. Montreal, Quebec: Callawind Publications, 1999.

London, Jonathan. *The Sugaring-Off Party.* New York: Dutton, 1994. [Picture-book account of maple sugaring in Canada.]

Stewart, Anita. *Great Canadian Cuisine: The Contemporary Flavours of Canadian Pacific Hotels.* Vancouver, BC: Douglas & McIntyre, 1999.

### Web Sites

Canada Day Cake Recipe. [Online] Available http://www.mochasofa.com/apps/recipes/RecipeDetail.asp?RecipeId=975 (accessed June 1, 2001).

Liboiron, Henri and Bob St-Cyr. "Making Pemmican." [Online] Available http://collections.ic.gc.ca/notukeu/pemmican_e.htm (accessed April 17, 2001).

Root, Lorna. "Food and More: Canadian Cuisine." [Online] Available http://www.geocities.com/lorna_lynne/recipes/recipe1.html (accessed April 17, 2001).

### Source for Special Ingredients

Always Canadian. [Online] Available http://www.alwayscanadian.com (accessed August 17, 2001).

# Canada
# French Canadians

## Recipes

French Pea Soup ........................................................ 70
Doughboys (Dumplings) ......................................... 70
French-Canadian Creton (Spicy Pork Pate) ................. 71
Butter Tarts ............................................................. 71
Tarte au Sucre (Sugar Pie) ...................................... 72
Pudding au Chomeur (Poor Man's Pudding) .............. 72
Tourtière (Meat Pie) ............................................... 73
Crêpes de la Chandeleur (Candlemas Pancakes) .......... 74
Ragoût de Boulettes (Spicy Meatballs) ....................... 74
Quebec Poutine ....................................................... 75

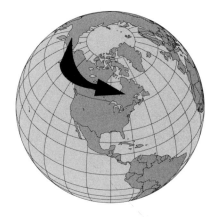

## 1 GEOGRAPHIC SETTING AND ENVIRONMENT

Most French Canadians (over 5 million) live in the province of Quebec. Most of the rest (about 1.5 million) live in the other northeastern provinces, known as the "Maritime Provinces" of Canada.

## 2 HISTORY AND FOOD

There are about 6.5 million French Canadians—descendants of French explorers and colonists—living in Canada. Most French Canadians (over 5 million) live in the province of Quebec. Most of the rest (about 1.5 million) live in the other northeastern provinces, known as the "Maritime Provinces" of Canada. French Canadians who live in the Maritime Provinces are often referred to as Acadians. There are small numbers of French Canadians living in the other provinces and territories, also.

Since the 1960s, interest in preserving French Canadian culture and traditions has grown. French Canadians share many common cultural practices: most are Roman Catholic, most enjoy food, art, music, and activities that began with their French ancestors. In 1974, French was recognized as the official language of Quebec, although English is the official language elsewhere in Canada.

## 3 FOODS OF THE FRENCH CANADIANS

Probably the best-known French Canadian dish is pea soup. It is enjoyed all over Canada, and is the traditional lunch (called dinner) on Saturday in Newfoundland, usually with dumplings called doughboys floating in it.

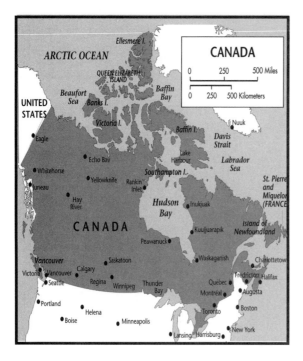

2. Measure the water into a saucepan and heat over high heat until the water begins to boil. Add the rinsed peas to the boiling water.

3. Lower heat immediately, and simmer peas until they are very soft (about 1 to 1½ hours). Add remaining ingredients and salt to taste and simmer for about 30 minutes longer, until vegetables are tender.

4. Make doughboys (if desired; recipe follows), or serve immediately.

Serves 8 to 10.

∞

## Doughboys (Dumplings)

*These dumplings may be cooked in the pot of pea soup before serving.*

### Ingredients

1½ cups flour

1 Tablespoon baking powder

½ teaspoon

¾ cup water or milk

### Procedure

1. Combine flour, baking powder, and salt. Gradually add the liquid until a soft dough forms.

2. Drop the dough by large spoonfuls into simmering soup, usually pea soup. Cover the pot tightly and simmer for about 15 minutes.

3. Serve bowls of soup with one doughboy floating in each bowl.

Makes 8 to 10 servings.

∞

## French Pea Soup

### Ingredients

10 cups water

2 cup dried yellow peas

1 small onion, chopped

1 carrot, chopped

1 stalk celery, chopped

1 potato, cut into bite-sized chunks

½ cup diced ham or 2–3 slices cooked bacon, crumbled

### Procedure

1. Measure peas into a colander and rinse well, picking out any discolored peas or pebbles.

## French-Canadian Creton (Spicy Pork Pate)

*Creton may be served as an appetizer before a festive meal or as a picnic snack.*

### Ingredients

1 pound ground pork

2 onions, chopped

2 cloves garlic, minced

1 teaspoon cinnamon

1 teaspoon cloves

1 cup dry bread crumbs

### Procedure

1. Combine the pork, onions, and garlic in a saucepan and cook over medium-low heat. Simmer, stirring frequently with a wooden spoon, for about one hour.

2. Add the cinnamon and cloves and continue simmering for about 20–30 minutes more.

3. Add bread crumbs and simmer for about 15 more minutes. (For a spicier mixture, more cinnamon or cloves may be added.)

4. Place a colander in the sink, and pour the creton mixture into it to drain off excess liquid. (Rinse the sink thoroughly, because the liquid may contain grease from the meat.)

5. Place the cooked creton in several small containers (such as empty margarine tubs or small bowls), packing the mixture down tightly.

6. Refrigerate. Serve cold as a spread for French bread or crackers.

Cory Langley

*Butter tarts are popular both for a snack or for dessert. While they are most common in Quebec, they can be purchased elsewhere in Canada.*

## Butter Tarts

### Ingredients

Pastry for double crust pie

¾ cup raisins

1 egg, slightly beaten

½ cup brown sugar

1 teaspoon vanilla

½ cup maple syrup

¼ teaspoon salt

¼ cup shortening

### Procedure

1. Preheat oven to 425°F (220°C).

2. Roll pastry out on a lightly floured surface. Cut into rounds with 4-inch round cutter. Fit the pastry into medium-sized muffin cups.

3. Put raisins into pastry shells, dividing evenly.

4. Measure all the other ingredients into a bowl and mix well to make the filling.

5. Fill each tart about two-thirds full with filling mixture, covering the raisins. Place muffin tin on bottom shelf of oven, and bake tarts for 12 to 15 minutes or until the filling is set.

6. Place tin on a wire rack, and allow tarts to cool. Remove from pan and serve.

Serves 12.

## Tarte au Sucre
## (Sugar Pie)

### Ingredients

Pastry for 9" pie, or frozen pie crust

2 cups brown sugar, firmly packed in the measuring cup

2 Tablespoons flour

Salt

2 eggs

1 egg yolk (discard egg white or reserve for other use)

1 cup milk

1 teaspoon vanilla

### Procedure

1. Roll out pastry and fit into 9" pie plate, trim and flute edges.

2. In bowl, blend sugar, flour, and salt.

3. In separate bowl using electric mixer, beat eggs and yolk till frothy; beat in milk and vanilla.

4. Stir egg mixture into sugar mixture till smooth. Pour into prepared pie shell.

5. Bake in 400°F (205°C) oven for 10 minutes; reduce to 350°F (175°C) and bake for about 35 minutes or till crust is golden brown and filling is set.

6. Allow to cool on rack.

Serves 6 to 8.

## Pudding au Chomeur
## (Poor Man's Pudding)

*Upside down cake with caramel base.*

### Ingredients for pudding (cake)

½ cup milk

3 Tablespoons butter, melted

2 teaspoons vanilla

¾ cup flour

1½ teaspoons baking powder

½ teaspoon salt

2 eggs

¾ cup sugar

### Ingredients for sauce

1½ cups brown sugar

½ cup chopped nuts (optional)

2 Tablespoons butter

Vanilla ice cream as accompaniment (optional)

### Procedure

1. Preheat oven to 350°F (175°C).

2. *Make pudding (cake):* Combine ½ cup milk, melted butter, and vanilla in small bowl.

3. Stir together flour, baking powder, and salt in medium bowl.

4. Using electric mixer, beat eggs and ¼ cup sugar in large bowl until thick and fluffy, about 3 minutes.

5. Add about one-third of the flour mixture to the egg mixture and stir to combine.

6. Next add about one-half of the milk mixture and stir to combine. Continue adding flour and milk, beating well after each addition. Set batter aside.

7. *Make caramel sauce:* Combine brown sugar and butter in a small saucepan and cook over low heat until butter melts and sugar dissolves completely.

8. Pour sauce into an 8-inch-diameter ceramic soufflé dish.

9. Spoon cake batter over brown sugar mixture in soufflé dish. Bake until tester inserted into center of cake comes out clean and syrup is bubbling at edges, about 40 minutes.

10. Serve hot with vanilla ice cream.

Makes 6 to 8 servings.

## 4 FOOD FOR RELIGIOUS AND HOLIDAY CELEBRATIONS

French Canadians celebrate holidays related to the Roman Catholic Church, especially Easter and Christmas. On Christmas Eve, families traditionally attend a religious service called a Mass (many attend Midnight Mass), followed by a festive holiday meal. One of the traditional dishes is a spicy meat pie called a *tourtière*, made on Christmas Eve using ground pork.

∽

## Tourtière
## (Meat Pie)

### Ingredients

2 Tablespoons vegetable oil

1½ pounds ground meat (traditionally pork for Christmas Eve)

1 onion, chopped

½ teaspoon allspice

½ teaspoon ground cloves

½ teaspoon ground cinnamon

1 Tablespoon Worcestershire sauce

2 potatoes, grated

Salt and pepper to taste

Pastry for double crust pie (may use pre-packaged pie crust)

### Procedure

1. Preheat oven to 375°F (190°C).

2. Prepare pastry (may use frozen or pre-packaged pie crust; recipe appears below).

3. Fit crust into pie plate and set aside.

4. Measure oil into a large skillet. Heat over medium heat for about 1 minute. Add onions and meat.

5. Cook until meat has lost all its pink color. Add allspice, cloves, cinnamon, Worcestershire sauce, and grated potatoes. Mix well, using a wooden spoon. Let simmer 5 minutes.

6. Fill pastry shell and cover with second crust.

7. Bake 30 minutes (until crust is golden). Serve hot. May be topped with ketchup or chili sauce.

Serves 6 to 8.

On February 2, French Canadian Roman Catholics celebrate the Fête de la Chandeleur (Candlemas), honoring the day in the church calendar when Mary took the baby Jesus to the temple, by eating crêpes (thin pancakes). A traditional French Canadian proverb says *"Manger des crêpes à la chandeleur apporte un an de bonheur"* (Eating crêpes on Candlemas brings a year of happiness).

## Crêpes de la Chandeleur (Candlemas Pancakes)

### Ingredients

1 cup flour

½ teaspoon baking powder

½ teaspoon baking soda

½ teaspoon salt

2 eggs

¾ cup milk

Vegetable oil

### Procedure

1. Break eggs into a large mixing bowl and beat with a wire whisk.

2. Measure flour, baking powder, baking soda, and salt into another bowl and stir to combine. Add gradually to egg mixture.

3. Add milk gradually, continuing to stir with the wire whisk. The batter should be smooth, with no lumps.

4. Pour oil into an 8-inch skillet to cover the bottom. Heat the oil over medium-high heat.

5. Using a soup ladle, carefully pour a ladleful (about ¼ cup) of the batter into the hot oil. Tilt the pan carefully to spread the batter into a large, thin crêpe that covers the bottom of the skillet.

6. Cook until the crêpe is golden brown on the bottom (about 3 to 4 minutes).

7. Carefully flip the crêpe over to cook the other side. Remove crêpe from pan, and blot on paper towel to remove excess oil.

8. Serve with maple syrup.

Serves 8 to 10.

## 5 MEALTIME CUSTOMS

French Canadians may eat a pastry, such as a croissant, for breakfast, accompanied by coffee or tea. For those with time for a heartier breakfast, eggs with Canadian bacon or sausage accompanied by toast and coffee. Lunch may be a ham and cheese sandwich made on crusty French-style or whole grain bread. Pea soup, served at home and in restaurants, is a favorite hearty week-end meal. Dinner may be *ragoût de boulettes* (spicy meatballs) or other meat dish, accompanied by potatoes, usually with gravy. Polite diners never put their elbows on the table until the meal is finished. Men may rest their forearms on the table, but women typically just hold their wrists against the table's edge while dining.

In Quebec street vendors and restaurants sell a quick snack called *poutine. Poutine* is French fries smothered in gravy and sometimes with melted cheddar cheese curds. Although this is not considered a traditional French Canadian food, *poutine* is a very common and popular snack or accompaniment to a casual meal everywhere in Quebec.

## Ragoût de Boulettes (Spicy Meatballs)

### Ingredients

¾ cup flour

¾ cup onion, chopped

1 Tablespoon olive oil

2 pounds ground pork (or combination of 1 pound ground pork and 1 pound ground beef or veal)

½ teaspoon cinnamon

½ teaspoon nutmeg

½ teaspoon ground cloves

1 teaspoon salt

¼ teaspoon pepper

3 cans beef broth (about 6 cups)

**Procedure**

1. *Make browned flour:* Measure the flour into a large skillet and heat over low heat. Stir frequently until flour is slightly browned. Set aside.

2. Measure oil into a skillet and heat over medium-high heat. Add chopped onions and cook, stirring frequently, until onions are translucent.

3. In a large mixing bowl, combine cooked onions, ground meat, and seasonings. With very clean hands, combine meat and seasonings thoroughly.

4. Shape meat mixture into meatballs about 1½ inches in diameter.

5. Pour broth into a large saucepan and heat to boiling. Drop meatballs into boiling stock, lower heat, and simmer about 1½ hours. (Cover pan with the lid slightly offset to allow some steam to escape.)

6. Sprinkle in the browned flour, a little at a time, stirring with a wooden spoon, until gravy thickens.

Serves 8 to 10.

EPD Photos.

*Poutine is a favorite snack for Canadians living in or visiting Quebec.*

∞

## Quebec Poutine

**Ingredients**

1 bag frozen French fries

8 ounces shredded cheddar cheese

1 jar beef or onion gravy (or packet of gravy mix)

**Procedure**

1. Prepare French fries in the oven according to the instructions on the package.

2. While the French fries are cooking, pour the gravy into a saucepan and heat it to just bubbling.

3. Remove the French fries from the oven, scatter shredded cheddar cheese over them, and return them to the oven for one minute, just long enough to melt the cheese.

4. Transfer the cheese-covered French fries to invidual plates or bowls, and drizzle with the gravy.

Serves 8 to 10.

## 6 POLITICS, ECONOMICS, AND NUTRITION

A major concern of French Canadians is the preservation of their French language and culture, since English is the dominant language in the rest of Canada and in their influential southern neighbor, the United States. A movement to separate the French-speaking province of Quebec from the rest of the country became a national issue in the 1970s; in 1980, voters defeated a proposal that would have granted Quebec its independence from Canada, but many French-Canadian separatists continue the campaign.

Canadians in general receive adequate nutrition in their diets, and the health care system is funded by the government, covering about 75 percent of health care costs for Canandian families.

## 7 FURTHER STUDY

### Books

Barbolet, Herb. *Farm Folk, City Folk: Stories, Tips, and Recipes Celebrating Local Food for Food Lovers of All Stripes.* Vancouver: Douglas & McIntyre, 1998.

Barer-Stein, Thelma. *You Eat What You Are: People, Culture, and Food Traditions.* 2nd ed. Toronto: Firefly Books, 1999.

Chavich, Cinda. *The Wild West Cookbook.* Don Mills, Ont.: R. Rose, 1998.

Claman, Marcy. *Rise & Dine Canada: Savory Secrets from Canada's Bed & Breakfast Inns.* 2nd ed. Montreal, Quebec: Callawind Publications, 1999.

London, Jonathan. *The Sugaring-Off Party.* New York: Dutton, 1994. [Picture-book account of maple sugaring in Canada.]

Stewart, Anita. *Great Canadian Cuisine: The Contemporary Flavours of Canadian Pacific Hotels.* Vancouver, BC: Douglas & McIntyre, 1999.

Tritenbach, Paul. *Traveling Taste Buds: Delectable Dishes from All Over the US and Canada.* Bishop, CA: Excellence Press, 2000.

### Web Sites

Always Canadian. [Online] Available http://www.alwayscanadian.com (accessed August 15, 2001). Online source of Canadian products.

Root, Lorna. "Food and More: Canadian Cuisine." [Online] Available http://www.geocities.com/lorna_lynne/recipes/recipe1.html (accessed April 17, 2001).

# Canada
# Aboriginals

## *Recipes*

Pemmican Cakes ............................................. 78

Saskatoon Berry Snack ................................... 79

Three Sisters Soup .......................................... 79

Bannock ........................................................... 80

Bannock on a Stick ......................................... 80

Man-O-Min (Ojibwa Wild Rice) ..................... 80

Wild Rice Cakes .............................................. 81

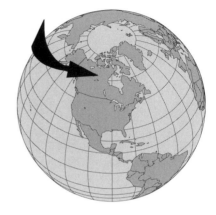

## 1 GEOGRAPHIC SETTING AND ENVIRONMENT

The phrases "Native Canadians" or "Aboriginals" describe the descendants of the people who were living in what is modern-day Canada before European colonists, explorers, and traders arrived in the 1600s. Giving labels to these groups is complicated by emotional and historical issues. Aboriginals inhabited all regions of Canada and the United States, and dozens of tribal groups, lived, hunted, fished, and foraged (gathered native plants) all across North America. The provinces of modern-day Canada obviously did not exist when the Europeans arrived on the east coast of Canada.

The Inuit inhabit the northernmost parts of Canada. On April 1, 1999, Nunavut (pronounced NOON-ah-voot) became Canada's newest territory, created from about half the land that made up the Northwest Territories.

## 2 HISTORY AND FOOD

In general, most Canadians agree that the approximately 800,000 Aboriginal Canadians counted by the 1996 Census of Population may be identified as belonging to one of three groups: First Nations (554,000), Métis (210,000), and Inuit (Innu, 40,000). The First Nations people are members of the approximately 50 recognized "First Nations" or tribal groups in Canada, and they inhabit all parts of Canada. The Métis are descendants of the intermarriages that occurred between the men employed by the early European fur trading companies (Hudson's Bay Company and Northwest Fur Company) and Native Canadian women.

The Inuit are the descendants of the Thule people who migrated from the Canadian arctic 700 to 800 years ago. They have been inhabiting the territory of modern Canada for thousands of years. They were historically hunters and fishers. Because of the

harsh climate of their northern homelands, the Inuit diet included very few fresh vegetables or fruits. In the short summers, they would gather berries, both for eating fresh and for drying to eat during the long, cold winter. They would also gather seeds and nuts to store to supplement the winter diet. Grains such as corn, wheat, and wild rice were harvested and dried. Grains would sometimes be ground to produce flour, or mixed with water and cooked.

Pemmican is a nutritious, high calorie food that can be prepared in quantities and stored. The French and English explorers, trappers, and traders, bought large quantities of pemmican from the Aboriginals, and even learned to make pemmican. Pemmican would be sealed inside an animal skin or stomach cavity to preserve it. Europeans carried these pemmican stores on long fur-trading expeditions.

## Pemmican Cakes

### Ingredients

1 package beef jerky

1 cup dried berries, such as dried blueberries, cranberries, or cherries

1 cup chopped nuts or sunflower seeds

¼ cup beef suet or vegetable shortening

Honey to taste (1 to 3 teaspoons)

12-cup muffin tin

### Procedure

1. Line muffin cups with paper liners (or grease cups well).

2. Grind or chop beef jerky into confetti-size pieces to make about 1 cup. Melt suet or shortening in a saucepan.

3. Remove from heat, stir in beef jerky, dried berries, and seeds. Stir in honey.

4. Spoon about ¼ cup of the pemmican mixture into each muffin cup. Press down firmly to make a cake, smoothing the top.

5. Refrigerate until well set.

Serves 12.

## 3 FOODS OF NATIVE CANADIANS

The traditional diet of Aboriginal people was made up of the animals and plants found on the land and in the sea around them. Seal, whale, buffalo, caribou, walrus, polar bear, arctic hare (rabbit), all kinds of fish and many species of bird were hunted or fished. Raw blubber (fat) was enjoyed or mixed with meat or berries. Every part of the animal was consumed or used to make clothing or shelter. Because the foods were eaten raw or with minimal processing, the

Aboriginal people were generally well nourished.

Modern-day First Nations, Métis, and Inuit people have added processed foods and convenience foods to their traditional diet, and are experiencing the health problems that come from consumption of foods rich in sugar and additives (such as tooth decay and obesity).

Their traditional diet was nutritious and high in calories, but the calories were needed to help keep their bodies warm through the long, frigid winters. During the short summers, Aboriginals (mainly the women) would plant small gardens and gather wild berries and seeds. Corn, beans, and squash were common vegetables grown in the small gardens of Manitoba and Alberta. These vegetables were often simmered to make soups or stews, such as Three Sister Soup (the "sisters" are corn, beans, and squash).

Snacks were often enjoyed right on the trail—a few berries or dried seeds plucked from the wild plants. Some were eaten right on the spot, and some may have been carried home to share or save for another day.

## Saskatoon Berry Snack

*Saskatoon berries, similar to blueberries, have been picked and eaten in the wild by Aboriginal Canadians for centuries. In the late twentieth century, commercial fruit growers began planting crops of these tasty berries to sell to grocery stores.*

### Ingredients

1 pint berries (may be blueberries, raspberries, strawberries, or other fresh berries

or

1 package dried berries (blueberries, cranberries, or other berries)

### Procedure

1. If using fresh berries, rinse them under running water.

2. Divide berries into several waxed paper bags or plastic baggies. Carry these along for snacks during the day or to share with a friend.

Serves 8 to 10.

## Three Sisters Soup

### Ingredients

3 cans chicken broth

2 cups frozen corn, thawed

1 cup green beans or yellow wax beans, washed and ends trimmed off

1½ cups of butternut squash (or pumpkin)

2 bay leaves

Salt and pepper to taste

Optional spices: ½ teaspoon red pepper flakes or 1 teaspoon each fresh (or ½ teaspoon each dried) parsley, basil, and oregano

### Procedure

1. Pour the chicken broth into a large saucepan or kettle. Heat until the broth begins to boil.

2. Add the corn, beans, squash, and bay leaves.

3. Lower heat and simmer for 45 minutes.

4. Add optional spices if desired, and simmer 15 more minutes.

5. Remove the bay leaves, and transfer the soup in batches to the blender to puree if desired. Serve with bannock (bread).

Serves 8 to 10.

Aboriginal peoples who lived on the prairies of western Canada consumed buffalo (and used buffalo skins for clothing and shelter). In central Canada, Ojibwa people would gather wild rice from the waters of Ontario and Manitoba, allowing it to dry and then roasting it. The fur traders, who came into contact with Aboriginal peoples all across Canada, introduced a bread similar to the Scottish scone. It became known as *bannock*. Bannock may be baked (Aboriginal people would lay it on hot rocks near a campfire) or twisted onto a stick and cooked over hot coals.

## Bannock

*Bannock may be baked in the oven or over a charcoal or open fire (recipe for Bannock on a Stick follows).*

### Ingredients

4 cups all-purpose flour

1 Tablespoon sugar

2 Tablespoons baking powder

½ teaspoon salt

2 cups milk (or water)

### Procedure

1. Combine flour, baking powder, sugar, and salt in a large mixing bowl.

2. Measure the milk (or water) and add it to the flour mixture, stirring with a fork to combine. A dough should form. If the mixture seems too dry and crumbly, add more liquid, one Tablespoon at a time.

3. Turn the dough out onto a surface lightly coated with flour. Knead for about 3 minutes. (To knead, press down the dough, turn it clockwise, fold it in half and press it down. Repeat.)

4. Preheat oven to 350°F (180°C).

5. Pat the dough into a circle about ¾-inch thick. Transfer the dough to a well-greased cookie sheet. Prick the surface of the dough all over with a fork.

6. Bake about 20 to 30 minutes, or until golden brown.

## Bannock on a Stick

### Procedure

1. Prepare Bannock dough (see preceding recipe). Have ready several sticks, 3- to 4-feet in length.

2. Divide the dough into balls slightly larger than golf balls. Shape each ball into a rope about 8 inches long by rolling it between the hands.

3. Wrap each dough rope around a stick. Hole the dough over a a bed of red hot coals (charcoal, wood, or gas grill flame set at medium.) Turn the stick frequently to bake the dough evenly.

Serves 10 to 12.

## Man-O-Min (Ojibwa Wild Rice)

### Ingredients

1 cup wild rice

4 cups

1 teaspoon salt

EPD Photos

*Wild rice, called Man-O-Min by the Ojibwa of central Canada, quadruples in size when cooked.*

## Procedure

1. Wash the wild rice in a colander or bowl, changing the water two or three times.

2. Measure water into a large saucepan; add salt. Heat the water to boiling.

3. Slowly add the rinsed rice to the boiling water. Lower heat to medium and simmer the rice, undisturbed, for about 40 minutes. (Do not stir the rice.)

4. The rice grains will swell to four times their original size.

5. Serve hot or at room temperature.

Serves 12.

Aboriginal peoples living in the region of modern-day British Columbia enjoyed foods such as salmon cooked over an open fire, a popular modern-day delicacy.

## 4 FOOD FOR RELIGIOUS AND HOLIDAY CELEBRATIONS

The traditional feasts held by Aboriginal peoples usually revolved around a harvest, or seasonal excess of food. For example, if there was a large salmon catch, a feast would be held. When a youth killed his first seal or caribou, a celebration feast might be held.

In western Canada, Aboriginal peoples held ceremonial parties called *potlatches* to celebrate the birth of a child, a young woman reaching puberty, or the marriage of a son. Modern-day potlatches are held to celebrate and preserve Aboriginal culture.

In 1996 an annual National Aboriginal Day was proclaimed, to be celebrated on June 21 each year. There is no specific menu associated with the celebration of this holiday, but many traditional foods, such as salmon, wild rice, and even buffalo, are enjoyed during the festivities staged by many of the Aboriginal groups.

## *Wild Rice Cakes*

### Ingredients

1 cup wild rice

4 cups water

1 teaspoon salt

¼ cup cornmeal

1–2 Tablespoons bacon drippings (or butter)

### Procedure

1. Rinse the wild rice in a sieve under cold running water and drain.

2. Measure the 4 cups of water into a saucepan and add rice and the salt. Heat until the water boils, reduce heat, and simmer for about 30 minutes. The rice should be tender but not soft.

3. Add the cornmeal slowly, stirring constantly with a wooden spoon and cook for 3 or 4 minutes. Remove from the heat.

4. Melt bacon drippings (or butter) in a skillet.

5. Shape the rice mixture into pattie-like cakes about 1½ inches in diameter.

6. Sauté the patties until they are brown on one side (about 5 minutes). Carefully turn the cakes over to brown the other side. Drain on paper towels.

Serves 12; may be served hot or at room temperature.

## 5 MEALTIME CUSTOMS

Aboriginal peoples are hospitable, and always have stews or teas simmering and available to serve to guests. Historically, cooking utensils were fashioned from natural materials and cooking was done over an open fire. Food preservation methods included smoking, drying, and encasing in melted animal fat or whale blubber.

## 6 POLITICS, ECONOMICS, AND NUTRITION

The substitution of packaged and fast foods for the nutrient-rich traditional Aboriginal diet has contributed to health problems among Aboriginal children.

The Canadian Government's Minister of Indian Affairs and Northern Development continues to work to address the concerns of the Aboriginal peoples. Addressing historic wrongs and developing modern-day programs is challenging, and representatives of the government and the First Nations, Métis, and Inuit peoples are striving to communicate and design goals to meet the needs of all Canadians.

## 7 FURTHER STUDY

### Books

Alexander, Bryan and Cherry Alexander. *What Do We Know About the Inuit.* New York: Peter Bedrick Books, 1995.

Bruemmer, Fred. *Arctic Memories: Living With the Inuit.* Toronto: Key Porter Books, 1993.

Harper, Judith E. *Inuit.* Mankato, MN: Smart Apple Media, 1999.

Jackson, John C. *Children of the Fur Trade: Forgotten Métis of the Pacific Northwest.* Missoula, MT: Mountain Press, 1996.

Lutz, Norma Jean. *Nunavut.* Philadelphia: Chelsea House, 2000.

Mercredi, Morningstar. *Fort Chipewyan Homecoming: A Journey to Native Canada.* Minneapolis, MN: Lerner Publications, 1997

Morrison, David A. *Arctic Hunters: The Inuit and Diamond Jenness.* Hull, Quebec: Canadian Museum of Civilization, 1992.

Santella, Andrew. *The Inuit.* New York: Children's Press, 2001.

### Web Sites

Aboriginal Awareness Week. [Online] Available http://www.aboriginalawarenessweek.gc.ca/ (accessed August 17, 2001).

Liboiron, Henri and Bob St-Cyr. "Making Pemmican." [Online] Available http://collections.ic.gc.ca/notukeu/pemmican_e.htm (accessed April 17, 2001).

Métis Nation. [Online] Available http://www.metisnation.ca (accessed August 17, 2001).

Métis Nation Ontario. [Online] Available http://www.metisnation.org (accessed August 17, 2001).

National Aboriginal Day. [Online] Available http://www.ainc-inac.gc.ca/nad (accessed August 17, 2001).

# Chile

## Recipes

Té con Leche (Tea with Milk) ....................................... 84
Ensalada Chilena (Chilean Salad)............................... 84
Pastel de Choclo (Corn and Meat Pie) ........................ 84
Tomaticán (Tomato and Corn Stew) ........................... 86
Cola de Mono (Chilean Eggnog)................................. 87
Torta de Cumpleaños (Birthday Cake) ........................ 87
Chancho en Piedra (Chili and Tomato Spread)............ 89
Barros Jarpa (Ham and Cheese Sandwich) .................. 89
Ponche (Berry Punch)................................................. 90
Arroz con Leche (Rice Pudding)................................. 90

## 1 GEOGRAPHIC SETTING AND ENVIRONMENT

Chile is located along the southwestern coast of South America. Chile is a 2,653-mile-long, skinny string of land, averaging just 109 miles wide. The country has the rugged Andes Mountains in the east and another lower mountain range along the coast of the Pacific Ocean. Between the two mountain ranges lies a fertile valley where Chile's agricultural activity is centered.

Around the main cities such as Santiago, the capital, and Rancagua, there is air and water pollution. Chile's main environmental problem is deforestation (clearing of forestland by cutting down all the trees), which leads to soil erosion. Chilean farmers do not grow enough crops or raise enough livestock to feed the country's population. Food must be imported, which is very expensive.

## 2 HISTORY AND FOOD

The Spanish came to Chile in 1541 and they brought grapes, olives, walnuts, chestnuts, rice, wheat, citrus fruits, sugar, garlic, and spices. They also brought chicken, beef, sheep, pigs, rabbits, milk, cheeses, and sausages.

Long before the Spanish came to Chile, the native Amerindians used corn in many of their dishes. The combination of the Spanish and Amerindians' foods formed popular corn-based dishes that are still part of the typical diet in the twenty-first century. Popular dishes include *humitas* (corn that is pureed and cooked in corn husks) and *pastel de choclo* (a corn and meat pie).

In 1848, many German immigrants came to Chile, bringing rich pastries and cakes with them. Italian and Arab immigrants also settled in Chile, along with other European immigrants. Each group brought its style of cooking to Chile. The Italians brought ices and flavored them with the different Chilean fruits. The Arab immigrants brought their use of certain spices and herbs, and the combination of sweet and salty tastes. Between 1880 and 1900, British immigrants brought tea to Chile. Teatime—inviting friends over for tea and coffee—continues to be enjoyed in modern Chile. Chileans serve *té con leche* (tea with milk).

## Té con Leche (Tea with Milk)

**Ingredients**

2 teabags

2 cups water

2 cups boiling milk

Sugar, to taste

**Procedure**

1. Heat 2 cups of water to boiling.
2. In a saucepan, heat the milk just to boiling, and remove from heat.
3. Place tea bags into 2 separate cups.
4. Pour the water into cups, filling ⅓ of cup.
5. Let the tea steep (soak) for 5 minutes, then remove bag.
6. Fill the rest of the cup with the hot milk.
7. Add sugar to taste.

Recipe may be doubled or tripled, to serve more guests.

Serves 2.

## 3 FOODS OF THE CHILEANS

Chile has a wide variety of foods, including seafood, beef, fresh fruit, and vegetables. A traditional Chilean meal is *pastel de choclo*, a "pie" made with corn, vegetables, chicken, and beef. This dish is usually served with *ensalada chilena* (Chilean salad).

## Ensalada Chilena (Chilean Salad)

**Ingredients**

4 cups onions, finely sliced

4 cups peeled tomatoes (may be canned and drained well), finely sliced

3 Tablespoons oil

Lemon juice, to taste

½ cup fresh cilantro leaves, chopped

Salt and pepper, to taste

**Procedure**

1. Place the sliced onions in a bowl.
2. Cover with cold water and let set for 1 hour, then drain the water.
3. Mix onions with the tomatoes on a large platter.
4. Season with salt and pepper.
5. Pour oil and lemon juice on mixture.
6. Mix and serve with chopped cilantro sprinkled on top.

Serves 4.

## Pastel de Choclo (Corn and Meat Pie)

**Ingredients**

4 cups frozen corn

8 leaves fresh basil, finely chopped (or 1 teaspoon dried, crumbled)

1 teaspoon salt

3 Tablespoons butter

1 cup milk

4 large onions, chopped

3 Tablespoons oil

1 pound ground beef

Salt and pepper, to taste

1 teaspoon ground cumin

1 cup black olives

1 cup raisins

2 pieces of cooked chicken breast, cut into cubes or strips

2 Tablespoons confectioners' sugar

## Procedure

1. Preheat oven to 400°F.

2. Heat the corn, basil, salt, and butter in a large pot.

3. Slowly add the milk, stirring constantly until the mixture thickens.

4. Cook over low heat for 5 minutes.

5. Set aside while the meat filling is prepared.

6. Fry the onions in oil until they are soft.

7. Add the ground meat and stir to brown.

8. Drain grease from pan.

9. Add salt, pepper, and ground cumin.

10. Use an oven-proof dish to prepare the pie. Spread the onion and ground meat mixture on the bottom of the dish, then arrange the olives and raisins on top.

11. Place chicken pieces over the top.

12. Cover the filling with the corn mixture, then sprinkle on the confectioners' sugar.

13. Bake in the oven for 30 to 35 minutes until the crust is golden brown.

14. Serve hot.

Makes 4 to 6 servings.

A typical Chilean dish is *cazuela de ave*, a thick stew of chicken, potatoes, rice, green peppers, and, occasionally, onions. *Humitas* are a national favorite, and they come from the Amerindians who are native to Chile. Humitas are made with grated fresh corn, mixed into a paste with fried onions, basil, salt, and pepper. The mixture is then wrapped in cornhusks and cooked in boiling water.

EPD Photos

*Corn husks wrap humitas, a favorite snack. Inside is a paste of grated corn seasoned with onions, herbs, salt, and pepper.*

*Empanadas*, little pies usually stuffed with beef, olives, and onions, are another favorite. A popular dish is *bistec a lo pobre* (poor man's steak), which is steak topped with two fried eggs, and served with fried onions and French fries. Despite the name, poor Chileans cannot afford to eat this meal because beef is very expensive; this dish is actually eaten by wealthier people. *Tomatícán* (tomato and corn stew) is often served as a side dish with meat, chicken, or fish.

## Tomatícán
### (Tomato and Corn Stew)

**Ingredients**

1 large onion, peeled and finely chopped

3 cloves garlic, peeled and chopped

2 Tablespoons olive oil

3 large plum tomatoes, peeled and diced

1 cup fresh or frozen corn kernels

1 pinch fresh parsley, chopped

Salt, to taste

**Procedure**

1. In a large saucepan, cook the onion and garlic in hot oil.

2. Add the tomatoes and cook, covered, for 5 minutes.

3. Add the corn and cook for another 3 minutes.

4. Add salt to taste, sprinkle parsley on top.

5. Serve hot.

Serves 4.

## 4 FOOD FOR RELIGIOUS AND HOLIDAY CELEBRATIONS

About 90 percent of Chileans are Roman Catholic, the religion that the Spaniards brought with them when they came to Chile in 1541. For Christmas, which occurs during the summertime in the Southern Hemisphere, families decorate Christmas trees, and on Christmas Eve they gather to eat a late meal. After the families eat, they open presents. Children enjoy *pan de pascua*, a Christmas cake made with fruits and nuts that comes from the German influence in Chile. During the holiday season, family and friends drink *cola de mono* (Chilean eggnog).

∞

## Cola de Mono (Chilean Eggnog)

### Ingredients

1 gallon milk

1 cup sugar

1 vanilla bean

1 cup whole coffee beans (or ½ cup instant coffee)

6 egg yolks

### Procedure

1. Bring the milk to a boil with the sugar, vanilla, and coffee.

2. Let it simmer slowly, stirring occasionally, until the milk turns a light brown.

3. Remove from the heat, strain, and return to low heat.

4. Add a couple of Tablespoons of the hot milk to the egg yolks to dilute and warm them.

5. Stir the yolks back into the mixture and cook for about 3 to 5 minutes.

6. Let it cool completely before drinking.

Serves 8 to 12.

Chileans also drink eggnog on New Year's Eve, celebrated on December 31. This is a favorite holiday. At midnight, Chileans hug and kiss each other, saying (in Spanish), "Good luck and may all your wishes come true." Some believe they will have good luck if they eat *lentejas* (lentils) at midnight.

Because many Chileans are Roman Catholic, days named after saints are important holidays. Children often celebrate the saint's day with the same name as theirs. October 4 is St. Francis of Assisi's day. Girls named Francisca and boys named Francisco celebrate this saint's day with a party and cake, as if it were their birthday. They also celebrate their own real birthdays. At both celebrations, *torta de cumpleaños* (birthday cake) is served.

∞

## Torta de Cumpleaños (Birthday Cake)

### Ingredients

1 box yellow cake mix (prepare the cake according to the package, using 2 round pans, 10-inch each)

1 cup grape jelly (another flavor may be substituted)

2 cups pastry cream (vanilla frosting may be substituted)

PASTRY CREAM:

2 cups whole milk

1 Tablespoon vanilla extract

5 egg yolks

1 cup sugar

½ cup flour

1 Tablespoon butter, melted

### Procedure

PASTRY CREAM:

1. Simmer the milk in a saucepan for 5 minutes and cover.

2. In a large mixing bowl, beat the egg yolks with the sugar until the mixture is light yellow.

3. Stir in flour, and pour the hot milk over the egg mixture, beating continuously with a whisk.

4. Pour the mixture back into saucepan and bring to a slow simmer, stirring constantly.

5. Lower the heat and cook for 2 minutes, stirring quickly.

6. Remove from heat.

Embassy of Chile

*Chile's long coastline provides ample opportunities for fishermen to gain access to the sea. Chilean cooks will often offer at least one dish featuring seafood for lunch and dinner.*

7. Add vanilla extract, and pour the cream into a bowl and spread melted butter over it.

8. Cover until ready to use

### ASSEMBLE THE CAKE:

1. Once the cake is cool, remove from the pans.

2. In Chile, each layer would be sliced horizontally into two separate layers, so that the cake has 4 layers in all.

3. This is an optional step; the cake will taste almost the same with just two layers.

4. Place one layer of cake on a plate, spread some pastry cream or frosting on it and follow with a layer of jelly. If us-ing more than two layers, alternate jelly and pastry cream or frosting between layers of cake.

5. Cover the top and sides of the cake with the remaining cream.

6. Let the cake sit overnight before eating.

Serves 8 to 12.

## 5 MEALTIME CUSTOMS

Mealtimes are an important part of family life. Families almost always eat together at home, only going to a restaurant on a special occasion.

Mothers prepare a light breakfast of toast and milk for their children. Lunch is the biggest meal of the day, and two main dishes are often served. The first dish might be a salad with seafood. The other dish might be *cazuela de ave*, a thick stew of chicken, potatoes, rice, green peppers, and, occasionally, onions. *Chancho en Piedra* (Chili and Tomato Spread) is often served with bread as an accompaniment to meals, or may be eaten by students as a snack. In small towns, businesses close for almost three hours so people can go home and eat lunch with their families and take a *siesta* (nap).

## Chancho en Piedra
## (Chili and Tomato Spread)

### Ingredients

4 garlic cloves, peeled and mashed

1 small jar chopped green chilies

1 small can chopped tomatoes, drained

1 Tablespoon olive oil

Salt, to taste (preferably kosher-style)

### Procedure

1. Combine garlic and chilies in a glass bowl, and "smash" together, using a wooden spoon. (Traditional Chileans would use a marble mortar and pestle to grind the ingredients together.)

2. Add salt.

3. Gradually add the tomatoes, mixing them well.

4. Stir in the oil.

5. Pour mixture into a small serving bowl.

6. Spread on slices of crusty bread or toast.

Sandwiches are a popular snack. Children can also take sandwiches to school for lunch. One popular ham and melted cheese sandwich is called *Barros Jarpa*, named after a Chilean who ate large amounts of these sandwiches.

## Barros Jarpa
## (Ham and Cheese Sandwich)

### Ingredients

1 Tablespoon olive oil

4 slices sandwich bread

2 slices cooked ham

2 slices Monterey Jack cheese

### Procedure

1. Heat the oil in a pan.

2. Place one slice each of ham and cheese on a slice of bread and place the other slice of bread on top.

3. Toast the sandwich in the pan on both sides until the cheese melts.

4. Serve.

Serves 2.

Restaurants range from snack bars to expensive restaurants. A favorite Chilean "fast food" meal is a *completo*, which is similar to a hot dog and typically accompanied with mustard, avocado, tomatoes, and mayonnaise. *Ponche* (Chilean punch) is a traditional and popular beverage.

EPD Photos

*Barros Jarpa (grilled ham and cheese sandwich), served with fruit, is a common lunch for students.*

Chileans also invite friends for teatime, a tradition from the British immigrants who came to Chile in the late 1800s. Dinner is usually one main dish. For dessert, Chileans eat fresh fruit, ice cream, or other desserts such as *arroz con leche* (rice pudding).

∞

## *Ponche (Berry Punch)*

### Ingredients

1½ quarts cranberry juice

½ teaspoon cinnamon powder

½ teaspoon nutmeg

6 whole cloves

1 lemon peel

1 orange peel

### Procedure

1. In a pot, simmer the cranberry juice with the cinnamon, nutmeg, cloves, and the lemon and orange peels for 15 minutes.

2. Let it cool and throw away the cloves and fruit peels.

3. Pour into glasses and serve.

Serves 4.

∞

## *Arroz con Leche (Rice Pudding)*

### Ingredients

1 cup rice

2 cups water

1 cup whole milk

2 large eggs

½ cup sugar

1 teaspoon vanilla extract

1 teaspoon grated lemon peel

1 teaspoon butter, for greasing the pan

1 cup heavy cream

Cinnamon to sprinkle on top

### Procedure

1. Preheat oven to 350°F.

2. Put the rice and water in a medium-size saucepan and bring to a boil over medium-high heat. Reduce to low heat and cover the pan.

3. Cook the rice for about 20 minutes, or until tender.

4. In a medium bowl, stir the milk, eggs, sugar, vanilla extract, and lemon peel until blended.

5. Add the rice and stir gently until all ingredients are well mixed.

6. Butter a 9-inch pie pan and spoon the mixture into it. Bake for 25 minutes.

7. Remove pudding from the oven, stir it, and cool for 15 minutes.

EPD Photos

*Arroz con Leche (rice pudding) may be served warm or chilled. A sprinkle of cinnamon adds just a hint of spice to complement the lemon peel in the pudding.*

8. While the pudding cools, beat the heavy cream in a large bowl until it forms soft peaks.

9. Fold the rice pudding into the whipped cream.

10. Serve in a dish, warm or chilled, and sprinkle with cinnamon.

Serves 4.

## 6 POLITICS, ECONOMICS, AND NUTRITION

According to a report by the World Bank, about 5 percent of the total population in Chile is undernourished, a decrease from nearly 15 percent in the early 1980s. A small percentage of children under age five show signs of malnutrition, such as being underweight or short for their age. Protein deficiency among the general population has induced an abnormally high rate of congenital (existing at or before birth) mental disabilities. Between 1994 and 1995, almost everyone had access to safe water and health care services.

One section of Chile's public health care system is called the National System of Health Services. It helps to provide periodic medical care to all children under six years of age not who are not enrolled in alternative medical plans. Through this program, low-income mothers can receive nutritional assistance for their children and for themselves. As a result of this program, the incidence of moderate to severe childhood malnutrition among those receiving assistance has been significantly reduced.

## 7 FURTHER STUDY

### Books

Bernhardson, Wayne. *Chile and Easter Island: a Lonely Planet Travel Atlas.* Hawthorne, Vic, Australia; Oakland, CA: Lonely Planet Publications, 1997.

*Chile.* Boston: APA Publications, 1996.

Galvin, Irene Flum. *Chile: A Journey to Freedom.* Parsippany, NJ: Dillon Press, 1997.

McNair, Sylvia. *Chile.* New York: Children's Press, 2000.

Novas, Himilce and Silva, Rosemary. *Latin American Cooking Across the U.S.A.* New York: Knopf, 1997.

Nurse, Charlie. *Chile Handbook.* Lincolnwood, IL: Passport Books, 1997.

Umaña-Murray, Mirtha. *Three Generations of Chilean Cuisine*. Los Angeles: Lowell House, 1996.

Van Waerebeek-Gonzalez, Ruth. *The Chilean Kitchen: Authentic, Homestyle Foods, Regional Wines, and Culinary Traditions of Chile*. New York: HPBooks, 1999.

## Web Sites

Embassy of Chile-USA. "Cultural Documents" [Online] Available http://www.chile-usa.org/culturaldocu.htm (accessed March 19, 2001).

SOAR: Searchable Online Archive of Recipes. [Online] Available http://soar.berkeley.edu/recipes (accessed March 1, 2001).

# China

## *Recipes*

Wonton Soup.................................................................. 95
Eggdrop Soup ............................................................... 96
Sweet and Sour Pork ..................................................... 96
Baat Bo Fon (Rice Pudding) ........................................ 97
Fried Rice ..................................................................... 97
Birthday Noodles with Peanut Sauce .......................... 99
Spiced Chicken ............................................................ 99
Almond Cookies........................................................ 100
Fried Wonton ............................................................ 101
Fu Yung Don (Egg Fu Yung).................................... 101

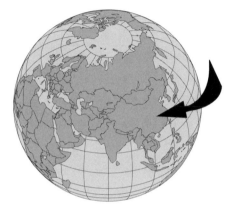

## 1 GEOGRAPHIC SETTING AND ENVIRONMENT

The official name of China is the People's Republic of China. Eastern China is made up of lowlands, whereas the middle and western sections of the country are mountainous. The largest river in China is the Yangtze, which travels almost 4,000 miles. Water pollution is a problem in China, but most Chinese people have access to safe drinking water.

About two-thirds of the population lives outside of the cities, but there are many people living in cities, too. More than sixty cities have populations over 750,000. Shanghai has over 14 million people, and Beijing has over 12 million. (To compare to U.S. cities: New York City has about 16 million people, Los Angeles has about 13 million, and Chicago has about 7 million.)

## 2 HISTORY AND FOOD

Throughout its history, China's growing population has been difficult to feed. By A.D. 1000, China's population reached 100 million (more than one-third of the U.S. population in 2000). The Chinese constantly had to adapt new eating habits because of the scarcity of food. Meat was scarce, so dishes were created using small amounts of meat mixed with rice or noodles, both of which were more plentiful. Vegetables were added, and stir-frying, the most common method of cooking, became a way to conserve fuel by cooking food quickly.

Regional differences in cuisine became noticeable in the 1200s when invaders from

**CHINA**

0    200    400    600 Miles

0  200  400  600 Kilometers

Rice is China's staple food. The Chinese word for rice is "fan" which also means "meal." Rice may be served with any meal, and is eaten several times a day. Scallions, bean sprouts, cabbage, and gingerroot are other traditional foods. Soybean curd, called tofu, is an important source of protein for the Chinese. Although the Chinese generally do not eat a lot of meat, pork and chicken are the most commonly eaten meats. Vegetables play a central role in Chinese cooking, too.

There are four main regional types of Chinese cooking. The cooking of Canton province in the south is called Cantonese cooking. It features rice and lightly seasoned stir-fried dishes. Because many Chinese immigrants to America came from this region, it is the type of Chinese cooking that is most widely known in the United States. Typical Cantonese dishes are wonton soup, egg rolls, and sweet and sour pork.

The Mandarin cuisine of Mandarin province in northern China features dishes made with wheat flour, such as noodles, dumplings, and thin pancakes. The best known dish from this region is Peking duck, a dish made up of roast duck and strips of crispy duck skin wrapped in thin pancakes. (Peking was the name of Beijing, the capital of China, until after the Cultural Revolution of the late 1960s. This traditional recipe is still known in the United States as "Peking duck.") Shanghai cooking, from China's east coast, emphasizes seafood and strong-flavored sauces. The cuisine of the Szechuan province in inland China is known for its hot and spicy dishes made with hot peppers, garlic, onions, and leeks. This type of

neighboring Mongolia swept into China. Cooking styles and customs began to be exchanged between the two countries. As people traveled further from their homes, cooking methods and foods were shared among the different regions within China.

## 3 FOODS OF THE CHINESE

The Chinese eat many foods that are unfamiliar to North Americans. Shark fins, seaweed, frogs, snakes, and even dog and cat meat are eaten. However, the Chinese follow the spiritual teaching of balance signified by yin ("cool") and yang ("hot"). This philosophy encourages the Chinese to find a balance in their lives, including in the foods they eat. While preparing meals, the Chinese may strive to balance the color, texture, or types of food they choose to eat.

cooking became popular in the United States in the 1990s.

Tea, the beverage offered at most meals, is China's national beverage. The most popular types of tea—green, black, and oolong—are commonly drunk plain, without milk or sugar added. Teacups have no handles or saucers.

## ∞
## *Wonton Soup*

### Ingredients

½ pound pork or beef, ground

1 Tablespoon scallions, finely chopped

1 egg, beaten

1 teaspoon salt

1 Tablespoon soy sauce

1 Tablespoon sugar

1 teaspoon sesame oil (optional)

1 Tablespoon water

2 packages wonton skins

3 cans (15 ounces each) chicken or other broth (about 6 cups)

EPD Photos/Cynthia Bassett

*A young Chinese vendor, with her hair styled in an elaborate bun, prepares vegetables to sell. All styles of Chinese cooking use fresh vegetables.*

### Procedure

1. Mix ground pork (or beef), scallions, egg, salt, soy sauce, sugar, sesame oil, and water in a bowl.

2. Place 1 teaspoon of meat mixture in the center of a wonton skin.

3. Moisten the edges of wonton skin with water and fold it to form a triangle. Press the edges together to seal.

4. Fill and fold the rest of the wonton skins.

5. Bring a large pot of water to a boil to cook the wontons.

6. In another pot, heat the broth. (Wontons will be cooked first in the boiling water and then added to the broth.)

7. Add a few wontons at a time to the boiling water, giving them room to float freely. Cook over medium heat 8 to 10 minutes.

8. Add the cooked wontons to hot broth. Use about 3 dozen wontons for 6 cups of broth.

Recipe makes 48 wontons.

∞

## *Eggdrop Soup*

### Ingredients

1 egg, room temperature

1 can chicken stock (about 2 cups)

½ teaspoon salt

½ teaspoon sugar

1 teaspoon soy sauce, thin

Large scallions cut into tiny circles (green parts only)

### Procedure

1. Remove the egg from the refrigerator and allow it to come to room temperature.

2. Beat the egg lightly in a bowl.

3. Put the stock in a saucepan or wok and bring to a boil.

4. Lower heat to the lowest setting.

5. Hold the bowl with the beaten egg above the pan with the simmering broth.

6. Slowly and carefully pour the egg into the broth in a very thin stream.

7. Hold a fork in your other hand, and trace circles on the surface of the broth, drawing out long filmy threads of egg on the surface of the broth.

8. Simmer for about 1 minute, and then remove the saucepan from heat and cover for 45 seconds.

9. The egg should be set in tender flakes.

10. Add salt, sugar, and soy sauce, and sprinkle the scallions on top.

11. Stir the mixture two or three times.

12. Transfer to individual soup bowls and serve.

Serves 2.

∞

## *Sweet and Sour Pork*

Note: This recipe involves hot oil and requires adult supervision.

### Ingredients

½ cup flour

½ teaspoon salt

½ teaspoon black pepper

1 pound lean pork loin, cut into bite-size pieces

3 Tablespoons peanut or vegetable oil

2 green peppers cut in large pieces

1 onion, sliced

1 carrot, sliced

½ cup pineapple chunks

½ cup pineapple juice

¼ cup white vinegar

2 Tablespoons soy sauce

¼ cup brown sugar

2 Tablespoons cornstarch

A few drops red food coloring (traditional, but optional)

Boiled rice, warm

### Procedure

1. Prepare rice according to package and keep warm.

2. Mix flour, salt, and pepper in a large plastic bag with a locking seal.

3. Add the pork pieces to the bag and seal.

4. Shake the bag well to coat each piece.

5. Remove the pork and throw the bag away.

6. Heat the oil in a large frying pan.

7. Cook the pork pieces on all sides until brown.

8. Lower the heat and cook for 20 minutes.

9. Add the peppers, onions, and carrots, and cook for 5 minutes.

10. Stir in pineapple, pineapple juice, vinegar, soy sauce, brown sugar, cornstarch, and food coloring.

11. Cook until the mixture is hot.

12. Serve over cooked rice.

Serves 4 to 5.

## Baat Bo Fon (Rice Pudding)

### Ingredients

¾ cup rice

1½ cups water

Pinch of salt

4 cups milk

½ cup sugar

½ teaspoon vanilla extract

### Procedure

1. Combine the rice, water, and salt in a large pot.

2. Heat until almost boiling, stirring often.

3. Lower the heat, cover pot, and simmer for 15 minutes, or until most of the water has been absorbed.

4. Stir in the milk and sugar.

5. Cook uncovered for 30 to 40 minutes, or until mixture is thick and creamy, stirring often.

6. Stir in vanilla.

7. Serve topped with sliced almonds, whipped cream, or a sprinkle of cinnamon.

Serves 6.

EPD Photos

*Ingredients ready for preparation of fried rice include (clockwise from top) chopped scallions, sliced mushrooms, bean sprouts, chopped red and yellow pepper, and sliced water chestnuts. In the bowl are three beaten eggs.*

## Fried Rice

Note: This recipe involves hot oil and requires adult supervision.

### Ingredients

3 Tablespoons peanut oil

4 cups boiled rice, cold

1 teaspoon salt

½ teaspoon black pepper

½ a green, red, or yellow pepper, chopped

½ cup mushrooms, sliced

¼ cup water chestnuts, sliced

½ cup bean sprouts

¼ cup scallions, chopped

3 eggs, beaten

½ cup parsley, chopped

**Procedure**

1. Cook rice according to instructions on package.
2. Allow to cool.
3. Heat the oil in a wok or skillet over high heat.
4. Add rice and fry until hot, stirring constantly.
5. Stir in salt and pepper.
6. Add the green pepper, mushrooms, water chestnuts, bean sprouts, and scallions, stirring often.
7. Push the mixture to the sides of the wok or skillet, making an empty space in the center of the rice mixture.
8. Pour beaten eggs into the empty space.
9. Let the eggs cook halfway through.
10. Blend the eggs with the rest of the rice mixture.
11. Heat until the eggs are fully cooked.
12. Remove the pan from heat.
13. Sprinkle the chopped parsley over each serving.

Serves 4 to 6.

## 4 FOOD FOR RELIGIOUS AND HOLIDAY CELEBRATIONS

Although day-to-day cooking in China is quite simple, elaborate meals are served on holidays and festivals. A typical holiday meal might consist of steamed dumplings, suckling pig (or a spicy chicken dish), and a selection of desserts. Unlike in the United States, desserts are generally reserved for special occasions only. Most ordinary meals end with soup.

The most important festival of the year is the Chinese New Year, which is set according the phase of the moon, and falls in January or February. Oysters are believed to bring good fortune and have become a tradi-tional food for dinners celebrating the New Year. Oranges and tangerines (for a sweet life), fish (symbolizing prosperity), and duck are also eaten. Dumplings are commonly eaten in the north. Neen gow, New Year's Cake, is the most common dessert. Each slice of the cake is dipped in egg and pan-fried. A special rice flour makes the cake slightly chewy.

Another important holiday is the Mid-Autumn Festival in September. To celebrate this festival, which occurs during the full moon, the Chinese eat heavy, round pastries

### Peking Duck Holiday Feast

Peking duck
Mandarin pancakes
Fish in wine sauce
Seaweed
Chinese celery cabbage in cream sauce
Pickled cabbage peking style

### Buddha Jumps Over the Wall Feast Menu

Buddha Jumps Over the Wall
(feast dish with as many as 30 main ingredients; takes up to 2 days to prepare)

Snow pea shoots with steamed mushrooms

Choi sum with yunnan ham

Mustard green stems in sweet mustard sauce

Lotus root with pickled peach sauce

called mooncakes. They are filled with a sweet paste and sometimes have an egg yolk in their center. Other foods eaten at this time are rice balls and a special cake called yue bing.

After a baby is one year old, the Chinese only celebrate birthdays every ten years, starting with the tenth birthday. The Chinese eat noodles on their birthdays. They believe that eating long noodles will lead to a long life. Another traditional birthday food is steamed buns in the shape of peaches, a fruit that also represents long life.

---

∞

## Birthday Party Menu

Noodles with peanut sauce
Honey-glazed chicken wings
Steamed buns
Almond cookies

---

4. Refrigerate the mixture until ready to serve.
5. Serve the noodles cold, topped with scallions, sprouts, or chopped peanuts.

Suggestion: Eat with chopsticks.

Serves 4.

---

∞

## Birthday Noodles with Peanut Sauce

### Ingredients

2 Tablespoons peanut butter or sesame paste, smooth

¼ cup hot water

3 Tablespoons soy sauce

1 teaspoon honey

4 cups Chinese-style noodles or spaghetti, cooked

2 scallions cut in ½-inch pieces (optional)

Bean sprouts (optional)

Chopped peanuts (optional)

### Procedure

1. Cook noodles according to package instructions and drain.
2. In a large bowl, use a fork to stir the peanut butter or sesame paste with the water until it is creamy.
3. Stir in the soy sauce and honey. Add the noodles to the peanut butter mixture and mix well.

---

∞

## Spiced Chicken

### Ingredients

3 pounds chicken pieces (may be chicken wings, boneless breasts cut into strips, or drumsticks)

¼ cup soy sauce

2 cloves garlic, crushed

1 teaspoon pepper

¼ cup sugar

2 Tablespoons vegetable oil

Several lettuce leaves

### Procedure

1. Rinse the chicken in cool water and pat dry with paper towels.
2. Mix the soy sauce, garlic, pepper, sugar, and oil in a bowl.

EPD Photos

*To make Almond Cookies, press a whole almond into the center of each dough ball.*

3. Thoroughly coat the chicken pieces with this mixture, reserving a little mixture in the bowl.

4. Let the chicken stand (marinate) for 2 to 4 hours in the refrigerator.

5. Preheat oven to 350°F.

6. Place chicken into a lightly oiled baking pan. Bake for about 40 minutes.

7. Every 10 minutes during roasting, turn the chicken and use basting brush to brush on the remaining soy sauce mixture. When the chicken is tender, remove from oven.

8. Arrange pieces on a bed of lettuce on a serving platter and serve warm or at room temperature.

Serves 6.

## Almond Cookies

### Ingredients

2½ cups flour

1 cup sugar

1 teaspoon baking soda

½ teaspoon salt

1 cup vegetable shortening

2 eggs, beaten

1 Tablespoon almond extract

About 48 whole almonds, unsalted

### Procedure

1. Preheat oven to 325°F. Grease cookie sheets.

2. Mix flour, sugar, baking soda, and salt in a bowl.

3. With a fork, slowly add shortening, a little at a time, to the flour mixture.

4. Add the beaten eggs and almond extract.

5. Shape the dough into balls the size of a large cherry.

6. Place the dough onto the cookie sheets and press an almond into the center of each cookie.

7. Bake for 25 minutes.

Makes about 4 dozen cookies.

## 5 MEALTIME CUSTOMS

Togetherness and cooperation is reflected in China's mealtime customs. A dish is never served to just one person, either at home or in a restaurant. Each person has his or her own plate, but everyone at the table shares food. Instead of a knife and fork, the Chinese eat with chopsticks, a pair of wooden sticks held in one hand. Food is cut into bite-size pieces while it is being prepared, so none of it has to be cut at the table. It is considered good manners to hold a bowl of rice up to your mouth with one hand. Chopsticks, held in the other hand, are used to help scoop the rice into the person's mouth. Drinking soup directly from the bowl is also an acceptable custom. It is rude, however, to leave chopsticks sticking straight up in a bowl of rice.

A typical family dinner consists of rice or noodles, soup, and three or four hot dishes. At a formal dinner, there will also be several cold appetizers.

A well-known type of Chinese snack is called dim sum ("touch of heart"). These are bite-size foods served with tea in mid-morning, afternoon, or at night. Typical dim sum are filled dumplings, shrimp balls, and spring rolls (also called "egg rolls" in the U.S.). Wontons, which can be boiled in soup, are also served fried as dim sum.

## Fried Wonton

Note: This recipe involves hot oil and re-quires adult supervision.

### Procedure

1. Prepare wontons according to recipe for Wonton Soup (or purchase packaged wontons).
2. Fry in hot oil until golden brown and crispy.
3. Drain the wontons on a paper towel and serve hot with duck sauce (sweet and sour sauce).

## Fu Yung Don (Egg Fu Yung)

Note: This recipe involves hot oil and adult supervision is required.

### Ingredients

8 large eggs at room temperature

1 cup peanut oil (used in varying amounts)

¼ teaspoon salt

Pinch of pepper, preferable freshly ground

¼ cup scallion, finely sliced (green part only)

½ pound cooked shrimp, each shrimp cut in half

### Procedure

1. In a large bowl, beat eggs with 1½ Table-spoons of peanut oil until bubbles start to form.
2. Add the shrimp to the beaten eggs and gently stir. Mix in the salt, pepper, and scallions.
3. Heat 2 Tablespoons of peanut oil in a wok or large skillet over high heat for about 20 seconds.
4. Tip the skillet or wok back and forth carefully to coat it thoroughly with oil.
5. Stir the eggs briefly once again, and pour the mixture into hot skillet or wok.
6. Cook the eggs, stirring gently with a wooden spoon until scrambled, about 3 minutes.
7. Turn off heat and transfer eggs to a heat-ed platter and serve. Sprinkle with scal-lions.

Serves 4 to 6.

## 6 POLITICS, ECONOMICS, AND NUTRITION

The rapidly growing population in China has been difficult to feed throughout history. About 13 percent of the total population in China is undernourished according a report issued by the World Bank in 2000. This problem is most significant away from coastal areas. People living in inland areas are more likely to be poor and to have a diet lacking in adequate nutrition. About 17 per-cent of children under age five are under-weight.

## 7 FURTHER STUDY

### Books

Albyn, Carole Lisa, and Lois Webb. *The Multicultural Cookbook for Students.* Phoenix: Oryx Press, 1993.

Beatty, Theresa M. *Food and Recipes of China.* New York: PowerKids Press, 1999.

Bremzen, Anya von, and John Welchman. *Terrific Pacific Cookbook.* New York: Workman Publishing, 1995.

Cook, Deanna F. *The Kids' Multicultural Cookbook: Food and Fun Around the World.* Charlotte: Williamson Publishing, 1995.

Foo, Susanna. *Chinese Cuisine.* Shelburne, VT: Chapters Publishing, 1995.

Halvorsen, Francine. *Eating Around the World in Your Neighborhood.* New York: John Wiley & Sons, 1998.

*Insight Guide China.* London: APA Publications, 1998.

Lo, Eileen Yin-Fei. *Chinese Kitchen.* New York: William Morrow, 1999.

Yan, Martin. *Chinese Cooking for Dummies.* Foster City, CA: IDG Books, 2000.

Yu, Ling. *Cooking the Chinese Way.* Minneapolis: Lerner Publications, 1982.

### Shops for Specialty Ingredients

Chinese ingredients can be found in many large grocery stores. Most cities have Chinese restaurants (where take-out versions of many recipes are available), and many have Asian specialty grocery stores. Look in the business pages of your local telephone book to find specialty grocery stores in your area.

Specialty Orient Foods, Inc.
43-30 38th Street
Long Island City, New York 11101
1-800-758-7634; [Online] Available http://www.sofi-ny.com/mail_order/english/mail_order_main_e.htm (accessed January 28, 2001).

The Oriental Pantry
423 Great Road (2A)
Acton, MA 01720
(978) 264-4576; [Online] Available http://www.orientalpantry.com (accessed January 28, 2001).

### Web Sites

Asia Foods. [Online] Available http://www.asiafoods.com (accessed January 28, 2001).

Chinese Cuisine with Rhonda Parkinson. [Online] Available http://chinesefood.about.com (accessed January 28, 2001).

# Côte d'Ivoire

## *Recipes*

Aloko (Fried Bananas).................................................. 104
Cornmeal Cookies ...................................................... 105
Fufu (Boiled Cassava and Plantains).......................... 106
Melon Fingers with Lime ............................................ 106
Kedjenou (Seasoned Meat and Vegetable Sauce) ...... 107
Baked Yams................................................................ 109
Chilled Avocado Soup ................................................ 109
Calalou (Vegetable Stew) ........................................... 109
Arachid Sauce ........................................................... 110
Avocado with Groundnut Dressing........................... 111

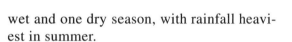

## 1 GEOGRAPHIC SETTING AND ENVIRONMENT

The Republic of Côte d'Ivoire (which means "ivory coast" in French), on the south coast of the western bulge of Africa, has an area of 322,460 square kilometers (124,502 square miles). Comparatively, the area occupied by Côte d'Ivoire is slightly larger than the state of New Mexico. The greater part of Côte d'Ivoire is a vast plateau, tilted gently toward the Atlantic, although the Guinea Highlands (in the northwest, from Man to Odienné) have peaks higher than 1,000 meters (3,280 feet).

The greatest annual rainfall, 198 centimeters (78 inches), is along the coast and in the southwest. The coastal region has a long dry season from December to mid-May, followed by heavy rains from mid-May to mid-July, a short dry season from mid-July to October, and lighter rains in October and November. Farther north, there is only one wet and one dry season, with rainfall heaviest in summer.

## 2 HISTORY AND FOOD

Thousands of years prior to the arrival of the Europeans in the 1460s, independent tribes occupied present-day Côte d'Ivoire. They survived mostly on gathered seeds and fruits and hunted animals. Foods and eating habits were most likely influenced by outsiders who used the land as trade routes from as early as the 700s. Little, however, is known about the early inhabitants.

By the late 1400s, the Portuguese began to show a significant interest in Côte d'Ivoire. They were interested in spreading Christianity, purchasing slaves, and discovering new trade routes. The Portuguese soon established several trading centers along the country's coast, but poor coastal harbors helped to spare the country from the build up of a large slave trade. However, the

**COTE D'IVOIRE**

Europeans desperately sought the country's supply of ivory (from the tusks of elephants) and gold, so trading and exploitation of these goods continued. The country's nickname, the Ivory Coast, originated because of the country's well-known supply of ivory. In return for the gold and ivory, the Portuguese brought European weapons and cassava, now a daily staple, to the Ivoirians.

By the mid-1800s, French merchants discovered the large amounts ivory and gold that originated from Côte d'Ivoire. In exchange for money and the promise of French protection, France was given permission to take control of the country's coastal trade routes. With the hopes of planting profitable cash crops (crops grown to make money), the French began planting coffee, cocoa, and palm oil (an essential ingredient for preparing African food) along the coast. Eventually one-third of the cocoa, coffee, and banana plantations belonged to the French.

As a result of France's push towards a strong economy based on cash crops, Côte d'Ivoire continued to mass-produce several crops after gaining its independence from France in 1960. Côte d'Ivoire is the world's leading producer of cocoa, and is the third largest producer of coffee in the world (behind Brazil and Columbia). More than one-quarter of the population works with the production of cocoa. Côte d'Ivoire also became Africa's leading exporter of pineapples and palm oil. Unfortunately, many of the country's rainforests have been destroyed in order to plant more cocoa (and other cash crop) plantations. Corn, rice, millet, and yams have also thrived, but mostly as crops eaten by the people of Côte d'Ivoire.

## Aloko (Fried Bananas)

### Ingredients

5 bananas

Oil

### Procedure

1. Cut the bananas lengthwise, then into little pieces.
2. Pour about 4 inches of oil into a saucepan and heat until boiling.
3. Place ½ of the sliced bananas into the oil.

4. Fry both sides until reddish-brown, then very carefully remove.

5. Fry the other ½, then remove.

6. Serve immediately alone, or with grilled fish.

Serves 4 to 6.

∞

## Cornmeal Cookies

### Ingredients

¾ cup margarine

¾ cup sugar

1 egg

1¼ cups flour

½ cup cornmeal

1 teaspoon baking powder

¼ teaspoon salt

1 teaspoon vanilla

### Procedure

1. Preheat oven to 350°F.

2. In a mixing bowl, beat margarine and sugar together until light and fluffy.

3. Add the egg and vanilla and beat well.

4. In a separate bowl, combine the flour, cornmeal, salt, and baking powder.

5. Slowly add the dry ingredients to the margarine mixture and mix well.

6. Drop dough in spoonfuls onto a greased cookie sheet and bake for 15 minutes.

Makes 3 dozen.

## 3 FOODS OF THE IVOIRIANS

Côte d'Ivoire's roughly 60 ethnic groups bring diversity to the country's cuisine. Each group has developed a diet that is suitable to their lifestyle. The Agni and Abron groups survive by farming cocoa and coffee.

The Senufo peoples live in the country's northern savanna (treeless plain). They cultivate rice, yams, peanuts, and millet (a type of grain). Rice with a peppery peanut sauce is often enjoyed by the Senufo people. The Dioula of the far northwest depend on their cultivation of rice, millet, and peanuts to survive, while the Kulango people of the north, who are mostly farmers, grow yams, corn, peanuts, and watermelons. Those living near the coast enjoy a wide variety of seafood.

Despite varying diets and food customs, the people of Côte d'Ivoire generally rely on grains and tubers (root vegetables) to sustain their diet. Yams, plantains (similar to bananas), rice, millet, corn, and peanuts (known as groundnuts in Africa) are staple foods throughout the country. At least one of these is typically an ingredient in most dishes. The national dish is *fufu* (FOO-fue), plantains, cassava, or yams pounded into a sticky dough and served with a seasoned meat (often chicken) and vegetable sauce called *kedjenou* (KED-gen-ooh). As with most meals, it is typically eaten with the hands, rather than utensils. *Kedjenou* is most often prepared from peanuts, eggplant, okra, or tomatoes. *Attiéké* (AT-tee-eck-ee) is a popular side dish. Similar to the tiny pasta grains of couscous, it is a porridge made from grated cassava.

For those who can afford meat, chicken and fish are favorites among Ivoirians. Most of the population, however, enjoys an abundance of vegetables and grains accompanied by various sauces. Several spicy dishes, particularly soups and stews, have hot peppers to enrich their flavors. Fresh fruits are the typical dessert, often accompanied by *ban-*

*gui* (BAN-kee), a local white palm wine or ginger beer. Children are fond of soft drinks such as Youki Soda, a slightly sweeter version of tonic water.

Often the best place to sample the country's local cuisine is at an outdoor market, a street vendor, or a *maquis*, a restaurant unique to Côte d'Ivoire. These reasonably priced outdoor restaurants are scattered throughout the country and are growing in popularity. To be considered a *maquis*, the restaurant must sell braised food (food that has been cooked over a low fire). The popular meats of chicken and fish are the most commonly braised food and are usually served with onions and tomatoes. Rice, *fufu, attiéké*, and *kedjenou* are also sold.

EPD Photos

*Cassava has a glossy, brittle skin, and is typically 6 to 8 inches long.*

## Fufu
### (Boiled Cassava and Plantains)

**Ingredients**

2½ cups cassava (also called manioc or yucca); do not use very center of cassava

5 plantains; do not use very center of plantains

**Procedure**

1. Prepare the cassava and plantains by peeling them, slicing them lengthwise, and removing the woody core. Then cut the cassava and plantains into chunks and place in a large saucepan. Cover with water.

2. Heat the water to boiling, and then lower heat to simmer. Simmer the cassava and plantains until tender (about 20 minutes). Drain.

3. Return the pan to low heat and pound, mash, and stir the mixture, using a wooden spoon or potato masher. Add a sprinkling of water to keep the mixture from sticking. Continue pounding and mashing for 15 minutes, until the mixture is smooth.

4. Form into balls and serve.

Makes 3 *fufu* balls.

## Melon Fingers with Lime

Melon Fingers make a delicious and refreshing dessert.

**Ingredients**

1 large honeydew, chilled

1 lime

**Procedure**

1. Cut the melon into eighths, or sections, about 1-inch wide and remove the seeds.

2. Next make cuts cross-wise about ¾-inch wide across each melon slice.

*To make melon fingers, slice a honeydew melon, remove the seeds, and make cuts across each melon slice.*

3. Arrange the slices on a large serving plate.

4. Section the lime and place a slice of lime in the center of each melon slice.

Serves 8.

∽

## Kedjenou (Seasoned Meat and Vegetable Sauce)

### Ingredients

2 chickens, cut into pieces

3 large onions, chopped

6 tomatoes, peeled and diced

1 piece ginger root, peeled

1 clove of garlic, crushed

1 bay leaf

Salt, to taste

Hot red pepper, to taste

### Procedure

1. Place the chicken, onion, tomatoes, ginger, garlic and bay leaf in a heavy casserole dish.

2. Season with the salt and pepper.

3. Cover with a thick, tight-fitting lid that will not let any steam escape.

4. Put the casserole on medium to high heat.

5. When the ingredients start to simmer, turn the heat down to medium to low.

6. Remove the casserole from the heat and without removing the lid, shake the casserole well to stir up the contents so that it cooks evenly.

7. Repeat this procedure every 5 minutes for 35 to 40 minutes.

8. Place the contents of the casserole on a warm platter and serve with rice.

Serves 8.

## 4 FOOD FOR RELIGIOUS AND HOLIDAY CELEBRATIONS

Most (65 percent) of Côte d'Ivoire's population follows traditional African religions. They honor their ancestors and believe in the spirits of nature. Even the other two major religions of the country, Christianity (12 percent) and Islam (23 percent), often combine traditional practices with their faith. Some traditional religions recognize sorcery and witchcraft, particularly those living in rural areas.

Probably the most anticipated time of the year for Muslims (believers of Islam) is Ramadan, a monthlong observance in which food and drink are not consumed between sunrise and sunset. *Eid al-Fitr*, the feast that ends this fasting month, lasts two to ten days. The feast may include a variety of seasoned meats with sauce, rice, yam or eggplant, salads, and soups or stews. *Eid al-Adha* (the feast of the sacrifice) starts on the tenth day of the last month of the Islamic calendar. After prayers, the head of each household typically sacrifices (kills) a sheep, camel, or an ox. It is often eaten that evening for dinner and is shared with those who could not afford to purchase an animal to sacrifice.

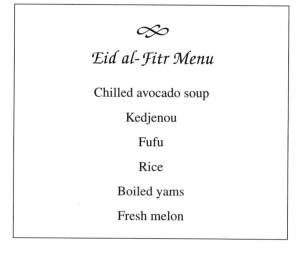

∞

*Eid al-Fitr Menu*

Chilled avocado soup

Kedjenou

Fufu

Rice

Boiled yams

Fresh melon

Christians, both Protestant and Roman Catholic, observe such holidays as Good Friday, Easter, and Christmas. Similar to the custom of Muslims on their special days, Christians gather with family and friends on Christian holidays to enjoy a meal together. Cities are often decorated with bright lights and decorations, and people gather in the streets to sell fruits and other items. *Réveillon*, the Christmas Eve dinner served after midnight mass, is often considered the most important meal of the year. A Yule log is traditionally eaten as a special dessert.

The people of Côte d'Ivoire also celebrate secular (nonreligious) holidays such as National Day (December 7), commemorating the country's independence, and New Year's Day (January 1). At the beginning of harvest time, yam festivals take place to honor the spirits who they believe protect their crops each year. To celebrate, the Kulango people exchange gifts and eat a meal of mashed yams and soup and participate in dances and song. Some villagers celebrate the harvest of other important crops, including rice.

∞

## Baked Yams

### Ingredients

5 cups yam pieces, boiled until soft

1 egg, beaten

1 Tablespoon butter, room temperature

Salt, to taste

1 egg yolk, beaten

Nutmeg and cinnamon, for dusting

### Procedure

1. Mash the soft yam pieces in a mixing bowl.

2. Gradually add the beaten egg, butter, and salt, mixing well to make sure that all ingredients are blended.

3. Spoon the mashed yam into an oven-proof casserole dish and spread the top with the beaten egg yolk.

4. Place it in the oven for 15 minutes, or until golden brown.

5. Sprinkle the top with nutmeg and cinnamon.

Serve hot. Makes 4 to 6 servings.

∞

## Chilled Avocado Soup

### Ingredients

2 ripe avocados, peeled and pitted

4 cups cold chicken or vegetable stock (2 14-ounce cans)

2 Tablespoons lime juice

1 Tablespoon plain yogurt

2 dashes Tabasco sauce, or to taste

Salt and pepper

4 paper-thin lime slices, for garnish

### Procedure

1. Add the avocado flesh to a blender and puree.

2. Add the stock and continue blending until smooth.

3. Blend in the lime juice, yogurt, Tabasco sauce, and salt and pepper.

4. Refrigerate for at least 1 hour.

5. When ready to serve, spoon into bowls and top each with a thin slice of lime.

Serves 4.

∞

## Calalou (Vegetable Stew)

### Ingredients

Cooking oil

2 to 3 pounds meat (red meat, poultry, or fish), cut into bite-sized pieces

2 pounds greens (traditionally cassava leaves, taro leaves, sorrel leaves; substitute mustard greens or spinach), stems removed and cleaned (note that taro greens must be boiled for a short time, then rinsed)

2 tomatoes, peeled and chopped

1 cup dried shrimp

Garlic, minced (optional)

Salt, pepper, or cayenne pepper, to taste

1 onion, finely chopped

### Procedure

1. Heat the oil in a large pot.

2. Fry the meat and onion until the meat is browned.

3. Add all the remaining ingredients and enough water to partially cover them.

4. Cover, reduce heat, and simmer on a very low heat for 2 or more hours.

5. Serve with rice.

Serves 6 to 8.

## 5 MEALTIME CUSTOMS

Some of the country's most tasty food can be found in people's homes. The Ivoirians are generous, hospitable people who enjoy inviting others to join them for a meal. Ivoirians believe that those who are blessed enough to be able to prepare a meal should share their good fortune with others.

In a typical village, villagers eat together in a common area. They believe eating not only gives the body nourishment, but also unites people with community spirit. Women and girls eat as one group, men as another, and young boys as a third group. Most villagers eat on a large mat placed on the ground. With their right hand (the left is considered dirty), villagers will scoop up their food from large bowls placed in the center of the mat for everyone to share. Most often rice is rolled into a tight ball and is used to scoop up meat and sauce.

The eldest villagers eat first. They do this in order to detect any contaminated or sour food. If bad food is suspected, the elder members will stop the younger members, including children, from eating from the bowl.

Once everyone has begun eating, there are some rules that are followed. It is considered rude and selfish to reach across the table for food. Villagers want to make certain that everyone receives similar amounts of food. Coughing, sneezing, and talking during the meal is discouraged. If a person needs to cough or sneeze, it is customary to get up and walk away from the mat before doing so. After the meal is over, a bowl of water is passed around to cleanse the hands. Talking amongst the villagers will typically resume as the diners relax to digest their meal.

∞

### Arachid Sauce

**Ingredients**

2 Tablespoons peanut butter

Water

4 pimentos (a type of pepper)

20 cherry tomatoes, mashed

Meat (beef, chicken, or fish)

Pinch of salt

1 Tablespoon oil

½ small onion

**Procedure**

1. Place the peanut butter in a pot and add 4 Tablespoons water.
2. Mix well until it is sauce-like and add 1 cup water.
3. Bring the sauce to a boil and add 2 more cups of water over a 25-minute period.
4. Add the pimentos.
5. Take 12 cherry tomatoes, remove the seeds, and mash.
6. Add the tomato mash and another 4 cups of water to the sauce and continue to boil.
7. After 50 minutes of boiling, add 2½ more cups of water, then let it boil again gently for 20 minutes.
8. Add precooked meat of choice and a pinch of salt and keep boiling for an addition 35 minutes.
9. Add the remaining cherry tomatoes, prepared as before, the oil, and the mashed onion.
10. Cook for at least 15 more minutes.

Serves 4 to 6.

∞

## Avocado with Groundnut Dressing

### Ingredients

2 ripe avocados (should feel soft when ripe)

1 Tablespoon lemon juice

2 Tablespoons peanuts, shelled

½ teaspoon paprika

½ teaspoon cinnamon

Cayenne, to taste

Salt, to taste

### Procedure

1. Peel the avocados and cut out the pit.

2. Cut the avocados into cubes.

3. Sprinkle with lemon juice and set aside.

4. Grind the peanuts roughly with a rolling pin or in a grinder for a few seconds.

5. Mix the peanuts and spices well and sprinkle over avocados.

6. Refrigerate until ready to serve.

Serves 4.

EPD Photos

*The ripe avocados for Avocado with Groundnut Dressing have pebbly black skin and creamy, soft flesh. The large pit in the center is easily removed.*

## 6 POLITICS, ECONOMICS, AND NUTRITION

About 15 percent of the population of Côte d'Ivoire is classified as undernourished by the World Bank. This means they do not receive adequate nutrition in their diet. Of children under the age of five, about one-quarter are both underweight and stunted (short for their age).

## 7 FURTHER STUDY

### Books

De Leschery, Karen, "More Fonio, Less Hard Work." *Aramco World.* January/February 1997: 38-39.

Sheehan, Patricia. *Côte d'Ivoire: Cultures of the World.* Tarrytown, N.Y.: Marshall Cavendish Corporation, 2000.

Webster, Cassandra Hughes. *Mother Africa's Table: A Chronicle of Celebration through West African & African American Recipes and Cultural Traditions.* New York: Doubleday, 1998.

*West Africa.* 4th ed. Victoria, Australia: Lonely Planet Publications Pty. Ltd., 1999.

## Web Sites

Ivoirian Cookbook. [Online] Available http://www.execulink.com/~bruinewo/recipies.htm (accessed April 23, 2001).

Ivory Coast Recipes. [Online] Available http://belgourmet.com/ (accessed April 23, 2001).

The Congo Cookbook. [Online] Available http://www.geocities.com/NapaValley/Vineyard/9119/c0088.html (accessed April 23, 2001).

World Travel Guide. [Online] Available http://www.wtgonline.com/data/civ/civ070.asp (accessed April 23, 2001).

# Cuba

## Recipes

Moors and Christians (Black Beans and Rice) ............ 114
Fried Plantains ..................................................... 115
Tuna in Sauce ..................................................... 117
Yucca (Cassava) .................................................. 117
Flan (Baked Custard) ........................................... 117
Helado de Mango (Tropical Mango Sherbet) ........... 118
Aceitunas Alinadas (Marinated Olives) ................... 119
Ensalada Cubana Tipica (Cuban Salad) .................. 119
Arroz Con Leche (Rice Pudding) ............................ 120
Crème de Vie (Cuban Eggnog) .............................. 120

## 1 GEOGRAPHIC SETTING AND ENVIRONMENT

The Republic of Cuba consists of one large island and several small ones situated on the northern rim of the Caribbean Sea, about 160 kilometers (100 miles) south of Florida. With an area of 110,860 square kilometers (42,803 square miles), Cuba is the largest country in the Caribbean. The area occupied by Cuba is slightly smaller than the state of Pennsylvania.

Cuba's coastline is marked by bays, reefs, keys, and islets. Along the southern coast are long stretches of lowlands and swamps. Slightly more than half the island consists of flat or rolling terrain, and the remainder is hilly or mountainous. Eastern Cuba is dominated by the Sierra Maestra mountains, whose highest peak is Pico Real del Turquino. Central Cuba contains the Trinidad (Escambray) Mountains, and the Sierra de los Órganos is located in the west. The largest river is the Cauto.

Except in the mountains, the climate of Cuba is semitropical or temperate.

## 2 HISTORY OF FOOD

Christopher Columbus discovered the island of Cuba on October 28, 1492, claiming it in honor of Spain. As colonies were established, the Spanish began mistreating and exploiting the native inhabitants of the island until they were nearly extinct. The colonists resorted to importing black slaves from Africa to operate mines and plantations. As a result, both Spanish and African cultures formed the foundation of Cuban cuisine.

Spanish colonists brought with them citrus fruits, such as oranges and lemons, as well as rice and vegetables. They also grew sugar cane, a major Cuban crop. African slaves were unable to bring any items along with them on their journey to Cuba. They were, however, able to introduce their African culture. The slaves developed a taste for fruits and vegetables such as maize (corn), okra, and cassava. In time, Spanish and African cultures joined together to create several popular dishes, including *arroz con-gri* (rice and beans, often known as Moors and Christians) and *tostones* (pieces of lightly fried fruit, similar to the banana).

Cuban cuisine, however, drastically changed after the Cuban Revolution in 1959. Fidel Castro overthrew the government. Cubans who opposed him began to flee the island, including chefs and restaurant owners. As a result, food shortages became frequent, and food that was still available was of poor quality. As of 2001, Castro was still in power and because of political disagreements with other countries, trade restrictions imposed on Cuba remain, so living conditions and shortages of food have improved little.

EPD Photos

*A favorite dish all year 'round is Moors and Christians made from black beans and rice. The name refers to the African (black beans) and Spanish Christian (white rice) roots of Cuban culture and cooking.*

∞

## Moors and Christians (Black Beans and Rice)

### Ingredients

1 pound black beans, dried (or 2 cups canned black beans)

1 large onion, diced

3 garlic cloves, crushed

3 teaspoons cumin, ground

½ cup green pepper, chopped

Olive oil, for frying

2 cups chicken broth

3 Tablespoons tomato paste

1 cup long-grain white rice

Salt and pepper, to taste

### Procedure

1. If you are using canned beans, drain the water from them and set them aside.

2. If you are using dry beans, cover them with water. Bring to a boil, remove from heat, and let stand 1 hour. Drain the beans.

3. Use a large, covered cooking pot and sauté the onion, garlic, and green pepper in the olive oil until tender.

4. Add the tomato paste, black beans, cumin, and chicken broth.

5. Add rice, cover and cook over low heat, stirring occasionally until rice if fully cooked (about 30 minutes).

6. Add salt and pepper to taste.

Serves 4 to 6.

∞

## Fried Plantains

*Note: Ripe plantains have peels that are almost completely black. However, the firm, ripe ones called for in this recipe are black and yellow.*

### Ingredients

4 firm-ripe plantains

Vegetable oil for frying

### Procedure

1. With a small, sharp knife, cut ends from each plantain. Slice through the peel and remove it.

2. Cut the fruit into very thin slices, about ⅛-inch thick.

3. In a large, deep skillet, heat oil (about ¼-inch deep) and fry 12 to 15 plantain slices at a time for 2 to 3 minutes, or until golden, turning them over once.

4. Use a slotted spoon or spatula to remove cooked slices and place them on paper towels to drain. Season the slices with salt. Plantain slices should be slightly crisp on outside but soft on inside.

5. The slices are best served immediately; however, they may be made 1 day ahead, cooled completely, and kept in an airtight container.

6. Reheat plantain slices on a rack in a shallow baking pan in a preheated 350°F oven for 5 minutes, or until heated through.

Serves 8.

## 3 FOODS OF THE CUBANS

Although Spain and Africa contributed most to Cuban cuisine, the French, Arabic, Chinese, and Portuguese cultures were also influential. Traditional Cuban dishes generally lack seasonings and sauces. Black beans, stews, and meats are the most popular foods. Root vegetables are most often flavored with *mojo*, a combination of olive oil, lemon juice, onions, garlic, and cumin.

Middle and upper class Cubans, including tourists, usually consume a wider variety of foods, if available. The most common meals include those made with pork, chicken, rice, beans, tomatoes, and lettuce. Hot spices are rarely used in Cuban cooking. Fried (*pollo frito*) or grilled (*pollo asado*) chicken and grilled pork chops are

EPD Photos

*Fried plantains, like white rice and black beans, are part of almost every dinner menu. In Cuba, the plantains would be fried in oil about one inch deep.*

typically eaten. Beef and seafood are rarely prepared, with the exception of lobster (which is so popular that it is becoming endangered in Cuba). Rabbit (*conejo*), when available, is also eaten.

Other common dishes in Cuba are *ajiaco* (a typical meat, garlic, and vegetable stew), *fufú* (boiled green bananas mashed into a paste) which is often eaten alongside meat, *empanadas de carne* (meat-filled pies or pancakes), and *piccadillo* (a snack of spiced beef, onion, and tomato). Ham and cheese is a common stuffing for fish and steaks, or is eaten alone. The best place to find the fresh-est fruits and vegetables on the island is at a farmers market. Popular desserts include *helado* (ice cream), *flan* (a baked custard), *chu* (bite-sized puff pastries filled with meringue), *churrizo* (deep-fried doughnut rings), and *galletas* (sweet biscuits).

Constant food shortages make finding or ordering certain foods nearly impossible. Economic hardship is another reason for poor food conditions. Cuba often trades its fresh produce, such as cassava, for money from other countries. This leaves a shortage of cassava and other produce in Cuba itself.

## Tuna in Sauce

### Ingredients

2 cans tuna, in oil

1 medium onion, chopped

1 medium green pepper, chopped

3 cloves of garlic, mashed

1 small can tomato sauce

1 teaspoon Tabasco sauce

### Procedure

1. Mix all ingredients in a saucepan and cook over medium heat, stirring constantly for about 10 minutes.
2. Cover, lower heat and simmer for 20 minutes.
3. Serve over white rice.

Serves 4.

## Yucca (Cassava)

### Ingredients

4 to 6 yucca (cassavas), peeled and halved

1 teaspoon salt

4 cloves garlic, minced

Juice of 1 lemon

½ cup olive oil

### Procedure

1. Scrape the peel from the yucca, and cut the yucca into pieces. Boil yucca in salted water until tender (about 25 minutes).
2. Drain yucca and add garlic and lemon juice.
3. Heat olive oil in a pan until bubbling, then pour over yucca. Mix well and serve.

Serves 4.

## Flan (Baked Custard)

### Ingredients

**FLAN:**

1 (14-ounce) can sweetened condensed milk

½ cup milk

½ cup water

4 egg yolks, beaten

1 teaspoon vanilla extract

**CARAMEL COATING:**

½ cup sugar

1 Tablespoon butter

2 Tablespoons water

### Procedure

**CARAMEL COATING:**

1. Measure sugar, butter, and water into a saucepan and cook over medium heat, stirring until bubbly and caramel brown. Be careful not to burn the mixture.
2. Pour into a warm baking dish, reserving a small amount to drizzle on top of finished flan. Roll dish to coat the sides completely with the caramel.

**FLAN:**

1. Preheat oven to 350°F.
2. Mix all flan ingredients and pour into a 2-quart baking dish that has been lined with a caramel coating (procedure above).
3. Place pan in a larger pan that contains water. Bake 55 to 65 minutes, or until pudding is soft set.
4. Chill. Drizzle caramel on top when serving.

∞

## Helado de Mango (Tropical Mango Sherbet)

### Ingredients

1 cup water

½ cup sugar

Dash of salt

2 mangoes, peeled and sliced

½ cup light cream

¼ cup lemon juice

2 egg whites

¼ cup sugar

### Procedure

1. In a saucepan, make syrup by combining the water, ½ cup of sugar, and dash of salt. Cook for 5 minutes on medium heat. Remove from heat and allow to cool.

2. In blender, combine mangoes and cream and blend until smooth and creamy. (If you do not own a blender, you can mash the mangoes with a fork and stir in the cream).

3. Stir in cooled syrup and lemon juice. Pour the mixture into one 6-cup or two 3-cup shallow pans and freeze until mixture is partially frozen (slushy).

4. Separate egg whites from eggs one at a time. Discard the yolks, or reserve for use in another recipe.

5. Beat egg whites to soft foamy peaks and gradually add the remaining ¼ cup sugar.

6. Place frozen mixture into a chilled mixer bowl, breaking partially frozen mixture into chunks. Beat until smooth.

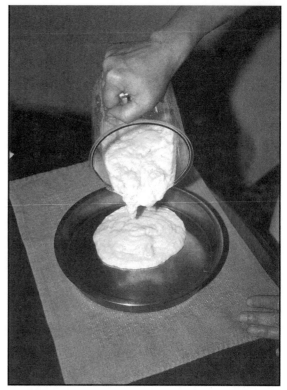

EPD Photos

*Pour the mango mixture from the blender into a pan. After the mixture becomes partially frozen, whipped egg whites will be added, giving the sherbet a lighter texture.*

7. Carefully mix in the beaten egg whites. Return mixture to freezing container and freeze until firm.

Serves 6 to 8.

## 4 FOOD FOR RELIGIOUS AND HOLIDAY CELEBRATIONS

Cuba is officially an atheist country (denies the existence of God or a higher being). However, it is estimated that about half of all Cubans are believers of a particular faith.

There are three general faiths that religious Cubans tend to follow: Afro-Cuban religions (saint worship), Judaism, and Christianity. For Christians, celebrating Christmas during the second half of the 1900s was often difficult. For years the government, ruled by Fidel Castro, did not encourage the celebration of a Christian holiday. However, the holiday of Christmas has been making a comeback since the end of the 1990s. Those who celebrate Christmas prepare a large meal on Christmas Eve.

A typical Christmas menu in Cuba might include *aceitunas alinadas* (marinated olives), ham spread, or ham croquettes (a ham-filled fried cake) for appetizers. Cuban salad, black beans, mashed plantains (*fufu*), Cuban bread, Spanish potatoes, white rice, yucca with garlic, and roasted pig may be a typical dinner. For dessert, rice pudding, mango bars, coconut flan, rum cake, Three Milks Cake, or Cuban Christmas cookies may be served. To accompany their meal, Cubans might drink Cuban eggnog, Spanish sparkling hard apple cider, or a Cuban rum and mint drink.

Some Cuban public holidays are January 1 (triumph of the Revolution in 1959); April 4 (Children's Day); May 1 (Labor Day); and December 25 (Christmas Day). During these days, grocery stores are usually closed and people often head for the island's warm beaches to celebrate, often packing food for the trip. On New Year's Eve, a small feast is prepared. At the stroke of midnight, twelve grapes are often eaten (in memory of each month) and cider is served.

## *Aceitunas Alinadas (Marinated Olives)*

### Ingredients

2 cups green Spanish olives, drained and unpitted

¼ cup olive oil

¼ cup red wine vinegar

¼ teaspoon ground pepper

3 cloves garlic, mashed

Freshly-ground black pepper, to taste

Peel of 1 lemon

Juice of 1 lemon

½ teaspoon cumin

### Procedure

1. Mix all the ingredients together in a glass bowl.
2. Cover and refrigerate for a minimum of two days.
3. Serve at room temperature. (This will keep in the refrigerator for several weeks.)

## *Ensalada Cubana Tipica (Cuban Salad)*

### Ingredients

2 ripe red tomatoes

1 head of iceberg lettuce

Radishes, sliced thin

1 white onion

#### DRESSING:

½ cup olive oil

2 Tablespoons white vinegar

2 Tablespoons fresh lemon juice

2 cloves garlic

1 teaspoon salt

¼ teaspoon pepper

**Procedure**

1. Cut the tomatoes into wedges.
2. Cut the onion in thin slices.
3. Break up the lettuce by hand.
4. Toss all the ingredients together with the radishes. Place all the vegetables in the refrigerator to chill.
5. In a separate bowl, mash the garlic with the salt and pepper.
6. Add the olive oil, vinegar, and lemon juice to the crushed garlic. Whisk together thoroughly.
7. Just before serving, gradually add the dressing, a little at a time, while you toss the salad with a large salad fork.
8. Add just enough dressing to cover the salad. Add more dressing, to taste.

## Arroz Con Leche (Rice Pudding)

**Ingredients**

½ cup rice

1 cup sugar

1½ cups water

1 quart milk

¼ teaspoon salt

1 lemon rind

1 teaspoon vanilla

1 cinnamon stick

Ground cinnamon

**Procedure**

1. Boil the rice with water, lemon rind, and cinnamon stick in a pot until soft, stirring occasionally.
2. Reduce heat to low.

3. Add milk, salt, vanilla, and sugar.
4. Cook over medium heat, stirring occasionally until thick (about 1 hour).
5. Sprinkle with cinnamon and serve.

Serves 8.

## Crème de Vie (Cuban Eggnog)

**Ingredients**

1 cup water

2 cups sugar

1 can evaporated milk

1 can condensed milk

8 egg yolks, beaten

1 teaspoon vanilla extract

**Procedure**

1. Before you begin, have a large bowl ready to fill with ice at the end of the cooking time.
2. Separate the egg yolks from the egg whites one at a time.
3. Combine the water and sugar and boil until it becomes syrupy.
4. Let cool.
5. In another saucepan, heat the evaporated and condensed milk and vanilla over low heat; do not let the mixture boil (if it starts to boil, take the pan off the heat right away.)
6. Add a little of the hot milk to the egg yolks to warm them.
7. Then very gradually add the egg yolks to the hot milk mixture.
8. Heat for about 5 minutes, stirring constantly with a wire whisk.
9. Remove pan from heat and put pan into large bowl filled with ice to chill the mixture.

10. While the mixture is cooling, add the syrup and mix well.

11. Strain the mixture through a coffee filter or a sieve lined with cheesecloth.

12. Pour into a pitcher or bottle, cover, and refrigerate until ready to serve. (Note: In Cuba, the egg yolks are added to cold milk and are not heated. Heating the yolk mixture thoroughly is recommended.)

## 5 MEALTIME CUSTOMS

A typical Cuban breakfast, normally served between 7 and 10 A.M., may include a *tostada* (grilled Cuban bread) and *café con leche* (espresso coffee with warm milk). The *tostada* is often broken into pieces and dipped into the coffee. Lunch often consists of *empanadas* (Cuban sandwiches containing chicken or another meat, topped with pickles and mustard). *Pan con bistec*, a thin slice of steak on Cuban bread with lettuce, tomatoes, and fried potato sticks, is also popular. Finger foods are popular snacks eaten throughout the day. *Pastelitos*, small, flaky turnovers (in various shapes) filled with meat, cheese, or fruit (such as guava), are also common snacks. Because Cubans are meat eaters, meat, chicken, or fish will normally be the main dish at dinner. It is almost always served with white rice, black beans, and fried plantains. A small salad of sliced tomatoes and lettuce may also be served.

Fast food establishments exist in Cuba, though popular U.S. chains, such as McDonald's or Burger King, have not yet set up restaurants on the island. However, a chain similar to KFC, called El Rápido, opened in 1995. *Burgui*, a chain similar to McDonald's, has restaurants throughout major Cuban cities and is open twenty-four hours.

Cuban restaurants are almost entirely government-owned. They have a reputation for providing slow service and bland meals. Privately owned restaurants, called *paladares*, normally serve a better meal, but are under strict government guidelines. *Paladares* are not allowed to sell shrimp or lobster, and are only allowed to serve up to twelve people at one table. However, most *paladares* serve these dishes anyway. Government-owned restaurants often try to disguise themselves as being privately owned to attract more customers. In Cuban restaurants it is common to have several menu items unavailable due to shortages of food. Some of the highest quality of food on the island is often found at expensive hotels that mostly serve tourists.

## 6 POLITICS, ECONOMICS, AND NUTRITION

About 19 percent of the population of Cuba is classified as undernourished by the World Bank. This means they do not receive adequate nutrition in their diet. About 9 percent of babies born in 1993 were considered to have low birth weight, a possible sign of inadequate prenatal (pregnancy) care. After the 1959 Cuban revolution and a decreased level of support from outside countries, some areas of social and health services began to fall behind.

Despite almost one-fifth of the population being undernourished, and a continuously unsettled economy, Cubans are in relatively good health. In 1993, nearly 100 percent of the population had access to free health care, and safe water was available to nearly all (95 percent) in 1995. Almost all doctors work for rural medical services after graduation, allowing rural Cubans to have nearly equal health care services as those who live in Cuba's larger cities. Having access to doctors and various health care services may help to reduce the cases of malnourishment in children.

## 7 FURTHER STUDY

### Books

Allan Amsel Publishing. *Traveler's Cuba Companion*. Saybrook, CT: The Globe Pequot Press, 1999.

Baker, Christopher P. *Moon Handbooks: Cuba*. Emeryville, CA: Avalon Travel Publishing, 2000.

Fallon, Stephen. *Guide to Cuba, 2nd ed.* England: Bradt Publications, 1997.

*Lonely Planet: Cuba*, 2nd ed. Victoria, Australia: Lonely Planet Publications Pty Ltd., 2000.

### Web Sites

Cuba Cultural Travel. [Online] Available http://www.cubaculturaltravel.com/religion.html (accessed February 22, 2001).

Cuban Food Recipes. [Online] Available http://icuban.com/food/ (accessed February 21, 2001).

CUBAVIP.COM. [Online] Available http://www.cubanculture.com/english/cocina.htm/ (accessed February 21, 2001).

Facts About Cuba: Cuba's History. [Online] Available http://icuban.com/facts/history.html/ (accessed February 21, 2001).

Three Guys from Miami: The Traditional Cuban Christmas. [Online] Available http://icuban.com/3guys/xmas.html/ (accessed February 21, 2001).

# Czech Republic

## Recipes

Houbova Polevka Myslivecka (Mushroom Soup)........ 124

Knedlíky (Czech Dumplings) ...................................... 125

Kure Na Paprice (Chicken Paprikas) ........................... 126

Fazolovy Gulás S Hovemzim Masem (Goulash).......... 126

Moravske Vano ni Kukyse (Cookies)........................... 127

Topinky S Vejci (Eggs on Toast)................................. 128

Mala Sousta Se Syre (Small Cheese Bites) ................. 129

## 1 GEOGRAPHIC SETTING AND ENVIRONMENT

The Czech Republic is located in the middle of Eastern Europe. It borders Poland to the northeast, Germany to the north and northwest, Austria to the south, and Slovakia to the southeast. The country was formally known as Czechoslovakia, and decided to end its union with Slovakia on January 1, 1993.

The land of the Czech Republic is made up of two regions. Rolling hills, plains, and plateaus make up the western region of Bohemia. The eastern region of Moravia is very hilly. Czech summers are relatively cool, with temperatures averaging 66 °F. Winters are cold, cloudy, and humid, with temperatures typically around 30°F.

## 2 HISTORY AND FOOD

Czech cuisine was influenced historically by the surrounding regions that dominated the country. In 1273, Count Rudolph, King of Germany, founded the Hapsburg dynasty. Eventually the dynasty controlled most of Europe, including the region of the present-day Czech Republic. The Germans brought with them roast goose, sauerkraut, and dumplings, which have since become Czech staple dishes.

In 1526, Ferdinand I of Austria began his reign as King of Bohemia (a western region in the Czech Republic) and the Hapsburg rule of Central Europe grew. From Vienna, the capital city of Austria, *schnitzels* (breaded and fried chicken or pork patties) were introduced to the Czechs.

Other culinary influences come from Hungary and Eastern Europe, whose people used present-day Czech Republic as a crossroad to other European countries. Hungary introduced *gulás* (goulash) to the Czechs, a meat-based dish served with dumplings, and

CZECH REPUBLIC

Eastern Europe offered such flavorings as sour cream, vinegar, and pickles.

## 3 FOODS OF THE CZECHS

Czech cuisine is considered heavy and very filling, with meals centered on meats and starches. This is because Czech winters are long and cold, which does not allow for a variety of fresh vegetables. In fact, if salads are available, they typically are limited to two vegetables, such as tomato and cucumber. *Houby* (mushrooms) are the exception, which flourish in local forests and are popular in soups, such as *houbova polevka myslivecka* (Hunter's mushroom soup).

Seafood is not widely available because the country is not located by any large bod-

ies of water. The fish, usually carp and trout, are raised in artificial lakes or fish farms. Some Westerners may think eating carp is unappealing, but in the Czech Republic, the water where they are raised is drained clean every year.

---

## *Houbova Polevka Myslivecka (Hunter's Mushroom Soup)*

### Ingredients

¾ pound mushrooms, sliced

1 onion, chopped

1 Tablespoon vegetable oil

2 strips bacon, cut into small pieces

¼ cup flour

5 cups water

1 chicken or beef bouillon cube

¼ cup heavy whipping cream

¾ cup cooking wine (or substitute water)

Salt and pepper, to taste

### Procedure

1. In a large pot, heat oil over medium heat.
2. Add the bacon pieces and fry until crispy.
3. Add the mushrooms and onion and fry until tender, about 4 minutes.
4. Add the flour and stir until the flour begins to brown.
5. Add the water and bring to a boil, then add the bouillon cube.
6. Stir until dissolved.
7. Reduce heat to medium and simmer about 20 minutes, stirring occasionally.
8. Add cream, salt, pepper, and cooking wine (or water).
9. Simmer for an additional 15 minutes.

Makes 4 servings.

Czechs eat a wide variety of meats, from pork, beef, *ryba* (fish), and chicken, to duck, hare (similar to a rabbit), and venison (deer meat). The meats are commonly served with *knedlíky* (dumplings), *brambory* (potatoes), or *rýe* (rice), and are covered in a thick sauce. Dumplings are popular side dishes, and are even stuffed with fruit as a dessert. The sauces are thick, like gravy, and are commonly made with wine. Sometimes fruit (such as cherries or berries of some sort), mushrooms, or onions are added for more flavor. Other common flavorings in Czech dishes are caraway seeds, bacon, and salt.

EPD Photos

*Knedlíky, or dumplings, are made from dough that is boiled in water.*

## ∞
## Knedlíky (Czech Dumplings)

### Ingredients

1 egg, beaten

½ cup milk

1 cup flour

⅛ teaspoon baking powder

1 teaspoon salt

4 to 5 slices white bread, cut into cubes

### Procedure

1. In a mixing bowl, combine beaten egg, milk, flour, baking powder, and salt until smooth.

2. Add bread cubes in batter and mix well.

3. Make 2 small balls from the dough.

4. Fill a large pot about half full with water and bring to a boil.

5. Drop the dough balls into the pot of boiling water and cook 10 minutes, then roll *knedlíky* over and cook an additional 10 minutes.

6. Remove immediately from the water and cut in half to release steam.

7. Serve with roast pork, sauerkraut, or *kure na paprice* (see recipe below).

Makes 4 servings.

One of the most popular dishes is called *vepro-knedlo-zelo,* which is roast pork served with *zeli* (sauerkraut) and *knedliky,* made by boiling (or steaming) a mixture of flour, eggs, milk, and either dried bread crumbs or potatoes. Another popular dish is *kure na paprice,* chicken made with a spicy paprika sauce. Sliced dumplings are used to mop up *gulás* (goulash) for a filling lunch or dinner. A Czech specialty is *svícková na smetane,* roast beef and bread dumplings in

EPD Photos

*Kure Na Paprice (Chicken Paprikas), a favorite Czech dish, is typically served with knedlíky (dumplings).*

3. Add butter to skillet. Sauté onion until softened, about 3 to 4 minutes.

4. Add remaining 3 teaspoons paprika and stir.

5. Add chicken broth to mixture and boil until sauce is thickened, about 8 minutes.

6. Place chicken back in skillet. Turn heat down to low and add sour cream, mixing to blend thoroughly. Season with salt and pepper to taste.

7. Serve with *knedlíky* (dumplings).

Makes 6 to 8 servings.

sour cream sauce, with lemon and lingonberries (similar to cranberries).

∞

## Kure Na Paprice (Chicken Paprikas)

### Ingredients

2 pounds boneless, skinless chicken, cut into chunks

4 teaspoons paprika

1 Tablespoon butter

1 Tablespoon olive oil

½ cup onion, chopped

1 cup chicken broth

¼ cup sour cream

Salt and pepper, to taste

### Procedure

1. Season chicken with 1 teaspoon paprika, salt and pepper.

2. Heat olive oil in skillet over medium to high heat and sauté chicken on both sides until thoroughly cooked. Set aside.

∞

## Fazolovy Gulás S Hovemzim Masem (Bean Goulash with Beef)

### Ingredients

1½ cups canned kidney beans

½ cup shortening

¾ pound beef, sliced

Salt and pepper, to taste

⅓ cup flour

2 Tablespoons tomato sauce

½ cup onion, chopped

½ teaspoon paprika

2 cups water

### Procedure

1. Heat beans in a large saucepan over medium heat until cooked through, about 3 minutes.

2. Add salt to taste.

3. Add the water and bring to a boil, then reduce heat to medium.

4. In a frying pan, heat the shortening over medium heat until it melts.

Cory Langley

*Two Czech children enjoy ice cream, seated on the threshold of a shop advertising two Middle Eastern favorites—shawerma (grilled, skewered meat) and falafil (deep-fried chickpea balls), with prices quoted in Czech currency, the koruny (Kc).*

## 4 FOOD FOR RELIGIOUS AND HOLIDAY CELEBRATIONS

More than 80 percent of the Czech Republic population is Christian, either Catholic or Protestant. Two of the biggest religious holidays are Christmas and Easter. Christmas Eve is celebrated on December 24 with a large dinner. According to one of the many Czech Christmas customs and traditions, a bowl of garlic is placed under the dinner table to provide protection to a family. There is an old superstition that if anyone leaves the dinner table early, they will die the following year. As a result, everything is prepared and placed on the table before anyone sits down so no one needs to get up before the meal is finished.

The traditional Christmas Eve meal is usually served around 6 P.M. and might include potato salad, soups, cookies, a fruit bread called *vánocka*, *koláce* (a type of pastry), and carp. Czechs go fishing for carp before Christmas Eve and usually keep the fish alive in the bathtub until it is ready to be prepared.

❧

## Moravske Vano ni Kukyse (Moravian Christmas Cookies)

*Moravia is an eastern region in the Czech Republic.*

### Ingredients

⅓ cup molasses

3 Tablespoons shortening

2 Tablespoons brown sugar

½ teaspoon each cinnamon, ground ginger, baking soda, and salt

1¼ cup flour, more if needed

5. Add the beef and onion and fry, about 4 minutes. Season with pepper.

6. Dust the meat with flour and allow it to brown.

7. Add a little water from the beans to the meat and onion mixture to make a paste.

8. Add this mixture to the saucepan of beans. Add tomato sauce and paprika.

9. Simmer for about 20 minutes on low heat.

10. Serve with bread.

Serves 4 to 6.

**Procedure**

1. In a large mixing bowl, combine molasses, shortening, sugar, cinnamon, ginger, baking soda, and salt.

2. Add flour, a little at a time, to form dough.

3. Cover with plastic wrap or foil and refrigerate for at least 4 hours.

4. Preheat oven to 375°F.

5. Divide dough into 4 balls, and keep covered with a damp towel.

6. On a lightly floured surface, roll each ball, one at a time, to about ⅛-inch thick (very thin).

7. Cut into desired shapes using cookie cutters or rim of a glass and place on greased cookie sheet.

8. Bake about 6 minutes, until lightly browned.

Makes about 24 cookies.

The food that is prepared for Easter dinner is usually taken to Mass on Easter Sunday, where it is placed on the altar and blessed by the priests. The blessed food is then taken home to be eaten. A traditional Easter dinner may include baked ham or lamb, *polevka z jarnich bylin- velikonocni* (Easter soup), made of different herbs and egg, and a loaf of sweet bread called *mazanec,* made with raisins and almonds.

## 5 MEALTIME CUSTOMS

A typical *snídane* (breakfast) in a Czech home is hearty–bread with butter, cheese, eggs, ham or sausage, jam or yogurt, and coffee or tea. For a quick breakfast, a Bohemian *koláce* (pastry) topped with poppy seeds, cottage cheese, or plum jam may be bought at a bakery.

### *Topinky S Vejci (Eggs on Toast)*

**Ingredients**

½ cup goat or cheddar cheese, grated

3 eggs

Salt, to taste

8 slices bread

2 Tablespoons vegetable oil

Paprika, to taste

**Procedure**

1. In a mixing bowl, beat the eggs.

2. Add the shredded cheese and salt.

3. Arrange the bread slices on a cookie sheet.

4. Cover the bread slices evenly with the egg and cheese mixture.

5. In a frying pan, heat the oil on medium heat.

6. With a pancake turner or spatula, pick up the bread slices one at a time and flip them mixture down, into the oil.

7. Fry the bread about 2 minutes, or until the eggs are cooked. Be careful not to burn.

8. When ready to serve, sprinkle with paprika. Serve immediately.

Serves 8.

*Obed* (lunch) is the main meal of the day for Czechs, where dinner may be no more than a cold plate of meats or cheese, such as *mala sousta se syre* ("small cheese bites"), and condiments. *Obed* is eaten between 11 A.M. and 1 P.M. Popular dishes may include *gulás* (goulash), *svícková,* roast beef in a creamy sauce topped with lemon and lingonberries (similar to cranberries), *smazený syr* (fried cheese), or *smázené zampiony* (fried mushrooms).

EPD Photos

*Mala Sousta Se Syre (Small Cheese Bites), slices of cucumber, cubes of cheese, topped with fruit, may be served as a snack or a light supper.*

∞

## Mala Sousta Se Syre (Small Cheese Bites)

### Ingredients

1 cucumber, thickly sliced

1¼ cups goat or cheddar cheese, thickly sliced

2 tangerines, peeled and sectioned, or 8 grapes

### Procedure

1. Place a slice of cheese on each slice of cucumber.
2. Pin a piece of tangerine or grape on top with a toothpick.

Serves 4.

Travelers may stop at a street stand and buy a *párek* (hotdog), *klobása* (spicy sausage), or *hamburgery*, which are not like Western hamburgers. A *hamburgery* is ground pork (not beef) with sauerkraut, mustard, and ketchup on a bun. Stands also sell Middle Eastern specialties such as falafil (deep-fried chickpea balls) and shawerma (grilled, skewered meat). Open-faced sandwiches called *oblozené chlebícky* are also popular, which are commonly made with cold meat, eggs, cheese, or mayonnaise-based salads, such as ham and pea, or potato. Sandwiches may be eaten with soups, such as *rajska* (tomato and rice), *polevka jatrovymi knedlicky* (soup with liver dumplings), or *polevka z hlavkoveho zeli s parkem* (cabbage soup with frankfurters).

Czech beer has been produced since the 1000s, and is considered some of the best in the world. Adults usually drink it at every meal, sometimes even at breakfast.

If there is room at the end of a meal, desserts such as *palacinky*, rolled crepes filled with jam, fruit, or topped with chocolate sauce, or *jablkový závin* (apple strudel) may be served.

Czechs prepare their foods in the kitchen and bring out the plates to the table. The head of the household or the guests are served first. The Czechs use their eating utensils to eat their meals. The *nuz* (knife) and *vidlicka* (fork) are kept in their hands throughout the meal and left crossed on the table to show that they are not finished eating. In many families, conversation while eating is minimal, unless there are guests. It is considered polite for a guest to bring inexpensive gifts to the children of a host.

## 6 POLITICS, ECONOMICS, AND NUTRITION

The Czechs have very few nutritional problems. Free assistance and care provided to women and children have resulted in a low infant mortality rate (number of infant deaths) of 7 per 1,000 live births in 1999. All school children are provided with medical attention, including X rays, and annual examinations. In 1997, children up to one year old were immunized for a number of diseases, including tetanus, and measles.

## 7 FURTHER STUDY

### Books

*Czech and Slovak Republics*. Melbourne, Oakland, CA: Lonely Planet Publications, 1998.

Martin, Pat. *Czechoslovak Culture: Recipes, History and Folk Arts*. Iowa City, Iowa: Penfield Press, 1989.

Martin, Pat. *The Czech Book: Recipes and Traditions*. Iowa City, Iowa: Penfield Press, 1981

Trnka, Peter. The Best of Czech Cooking. New York, NY: Hippocrene Books, 1996.

### Web Sites

Diana's Gourmet Corner. [Online] Available http://belgourmet.com/cooking/links/cze.html (accessed April 17, 2001).

Locallingo.com. [Online] Available http://www.locallingo.com/countries/czech_republic/culture/easter.html (accessed April 17, 2001).

The Prague Post. [Online] Available http://www.praguepost.cz/tourist/tourfood.html (accessed April 17, 2001).

Radio Czech. [Online] Available http://www.radio.cz/christmas/customs.html (accessed April 17, 2001).

# Egypt

## *Recipes*

Ful Mudammas (Broad Beans in Sauce) ..................... 132

Koushari (Lentils, Macaroni, Rice, and Chickpeas) ...... 133

Shai (Mint Tea) and Baklava ....................................... 134

Lemon and Garlic Potato Salad ................................. 135

Gebna Makleyah (Oven-Fried Cheese) ..................... 135

Bamia (Sweet and Sour Okra) .................................... 137

'Irea (Cinnamon Beverage) ........................................ 138

Khoshaf ....................................................................... 138

Lettuce Salad .............................................................. 138

Spinach with Garlic .................................................... 139

## 1 GEOGRAPHIC SETTING AND ENVIRONMENT

The Arab Republic of Egypt is located in the northeastern region of the African continent, bordering both the Mediterranean and Red Seas. The climate is arid and dry and most of the country receives less than one inch of rainfall each year. The Mediterranean may offer Egypt's northern coastline up to eight inches of rainfall each year, and keeps year-round temperatures cooler than the inland deserts. The widespread lack of rainfall makes it extremely difficult to grow crops. Egypt has no forests and only 2 percent of the land is arable (land that can be farmed).

The well-known Nile River, the longest river in the world, runs north and south through eastern Egypt and empties into the Mediterranean Sea. The Nile River Valley, which includes the capital city of Cairo, is the most fertile land in Egypt. Approximately 95 percent of the country's population lives alongside the Nile River. However, overcrowding in this region is threatening Egypt's wildlife and endangering the Nile's water supply.

## 2 HISTORY AND FOOD

Thousands of years ago, ancient Egyptians left evidence of their love for food. Well-preserved wall paintings and carvings have been discovered on tombs and temples, depicting large feasts and a variety of foods. Many of these ancient foods are still eaten in Egyptian households today. Peas, beans, cucumbers, dates, figs, and grapes were popular fruits and vegetables in ancient times. Wheat and barley, ancient staple crops, were used to make bread and beer. Fish and poultry were also popular. Dried

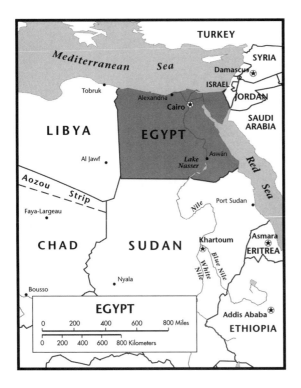

tains its uniqueness. After thousands of years, rice and bread remain staple foods, and *molokhiyya* (a spinach-like vegetable) and *ful mudammas* (cooked, creamy fava beans), a national dish, are nearly as popular as long ago.

## Ful Mudammas (Broad Beans in Sauce)

### Ingredients

2 cans (15-ounce each) cooked fava beans

6 cloves garlic, or to taste

1 teaspoon salt, or to taste

1 Tablespoon lemon juice, freshly squeezed

¼ cup olive oil

1½ Tablespoons parsley, minced

Garnish, such as radishes, hard-boiled eggs, chopped scallions, pita bread (toasted and cut into wedges)

### Procedure

1. Press the garlic cloves through a garlic press into a medium bowl.

2. Mash the garlic and salt together.

3. Next, add the lemon juice, olive oil, and parsley to the garlic mixture and combine thoroughly.

4. Drain the beans well, rinse, and put beans into a large pot over low heat.

5. Add garlic mixture and stir with a wooden spoon to combine thoroughly.

6. Serve warm with the garnishes arranged on a platter.

7. Each person is served a plateful of *Ful Mudammas* and adds the garnishes of his or her choice.

Serves 4 to 6.

fish was prepared by cleaning the fish, coating the pieces with salt, and placing them the sun to dry. *Fasieekh* (salted, dried fish) remained a popular meal in Egypt as of 2000.

The unique Egyptian cuisine has been influenced throughout history, particularly by its neighbors from the Middle East. Persians (modern-day Iraqis), Greeks, Romans (modern-day Italians), Arabs, and Ottomans (from modern-day Turkey) first influenced Egyptian cuisine thousands of years ago. More recently, the foods of other Arabic people in the Middle East such as the Lebanese, Palestinians, Syrians, as well as some foods from Europe, have affected the Egyptian diet. However, Egyptian cuisine main-

EPD Photos

*Koushari, a vegetarian dish, combines lentils, chick peas, macaroni, and rice in a tomato sauce subtly flavored with onions and garlic. It is always accompanied by pita bread.*

## 3 FOODS OF THE EGYPTIANS

Egypt has a variety of national dishes. *Ful* (pronounced "fool," bean paste), *tahini* (sesame paste), *koushari* (lentils, macaroni, rice, and chickpeas), *aish baladi* (a pita-like bread), *kofta* (spicy, minced lamb), and *kebab* (grilled lamb pieces) are the most popular.

∞

### Koushari
### (Lentils, Macaroni, Rice, and Chickpeas)

#### Ingredients

1 cup lentils

1 teaspoon salt

1 cup elbow macaroni

1 cup rice

1 can (15-ounce) chickpeas (also called ceci)

2 Tablespoons olive oil

**SAUCE:**

1 cup canned tomato puree

¼ cup olive oil

2 onions

1 garlic clove, or to taste

#### Procedure

1. *Prepare lentils:* Place the lentils in a sieve and rinse thoroughly. Place them in a large saucepan with 3 cups of water and 1 teaspoon salt.

2. Heat until the water begins to boil. Lower the heat, and simmer for about 1 hour until lentils are tender. Drain and set the lentils aside.

3. *Prepare the macaroni:* Fill the same saucepan with water (add salt if desired). Heat until the water begins to boil.

4. Add the macaroni and boil about 12 to 15 minutes, until macaroni is tender. Drain and set the macaroni aside. (It is okay to combine the macaroni and lentils.)

5. *Prepare the rice:* Heat the 2 Tablespoons of olive oil in the same saucepan. Add the rice and cook for 2 or 3 minutes, thoroughly coating the rice with oil.

6. Add 2 cups of water and heat until the water begins to boil. Cover the saucepan and simmer until the rice is tender, about 15 minutes.

7. Remove from heat and allow to cool for about 5 minutes.

8. *Assemble koushari:* Drain chickpeas and rinse. Add chickpeas, lentils, and macaroni to cooked rice and toss very gently with a fork.

9. *Make sauce:* Peel the onions and cut them in half lengthwise. Slice each half crosswise into thin slices.

10. Heat ¼ cup olive oil in a skillet. Add onions and cook, stirring often with a wooden spoon, until onions are golden brown.

11. Add garlic clove and cook 1 or 2 more minutes. Stir in tomato puree and heat until bubbly.

12. Now pour the sauce over the lentil mixture and heat over very low heat for about 5 minutes, until completely warm.

13. Serve with pita bread.

Serves 4 to 6.

*Aish*, the Arabic name for bread, means "life." It accompanies most meals and is served in various forms. The most common bread is pita, usually made with whole wheat (or sometimes white) flour. Long, skinny French-style loaves of bread are also widely eaten throughout the country. Traditional Egyptian cheeses, as well as feta imported from neighboring Greece, are frequently served alongside bread at meals.

Despite the country's dry climate and shortage of arable land (land that can be farmed), Egypt grows a variety of fresh fruits. *Mohz* (bananas), *balah* (dates), *burtu'aan* (oranges), *battiikh* (melon), *khukh* (peaches), *berkuk* (plums), and *'anub* (grapes) are commonly grown.

*Ful* (creamy bean paste made from fava beans), one of the country's several national dishes, is a typical breakfast meal. It is often served in a spicy sauce, topped with an egg. Lunch, normally served between 2 P.M. and 4 P.M., usually includes meat or fish, rice, bread, and seasonal vegetables. Salad (*mezza,* or *mezze* if more than one is served), topped with typical Middle Eastern fare such as olives, cheese, and nuts, may also be eaten. Meat (usually lamb, chicken, fish, rabbit, or pigeon), vegetables, and bread make up a typical dinner in Egypt. Tea and a dessert, such as *baklava* (honey pastry), *basbousa* (cream-filled cake), or *konafa* (cooked batter stuffed with nuts), are familiar after-dinner treats.

Tea and coffee are widely consumed. Egypt's numerous coffee and teahouses brew very strong coffee and tea (often mint tea), usually offering both full of sugar. Coffeehouses are typically filled with men who gather to play dominoes or backgammon. Coffee is served *saada* or "bitter" (no sugar) or *ziyada* or "very sweet." Egyptians also enjoy a drink called sahleb, made from wheat, milk, and chopped nuts.

For a typical dessert, Egyptians may serve mint tea with sugar and a sweet, flaky pastry called baklava.

∞

## *Shai (Mint Tea) and Baklava*

### Ingredients

1 package mint tea (loose or in tea bags)

Sugar

4 to 6 cups water (depending on how many people are being served)

### Procedure

1. Bring water to a boil.
2. If using loose tea, measure 1 teaspoon of tea leaves into a teapot for each person being served.
3. Otherwise, place one tea bag per person into the teapot.
4. Pour boiling water over tea.
5. Allow to steep (soak) for about 3 minutes.
6. Pour tea into cups. (In Egypt, small glass tumblers are used.)
7. If loose tea is used, allow the tea leaves to settle to the bottom of the pot, and pour carefully to avoid disturbing them.

8. Add 4 or 5 teaspoonful of sugar to each cup.

9. Enjoy with a piece of baklava, purchased from a bakery.

Serves 4 to 6.

∞

## Lemon and Garlic Potato Salad

### Ingredients

2 pounds of red potatoes, scrubbed but with skin left on

½ cup parsley, chopped

4 garlic cloves, minced

Juice of 1½ lemons

1 Tablespoon vegetable oil

Salt and pepper, to taste

EPD Photos

*Cheese with bread is frequently served at meals. Here, oven-fried cheese, Gebna Makleyah (recipe follows), is served with lemon wedges and pita triangles.*

### Procedure

1. Boil potatoes until tender (½ hour to 1 hour, or until a fork can easily pierce the skin) and let cool.

2. Add parsley, garlic cloves, lemon juice, oil, and salt and pepper; mix well.

3. Chill and serve.

Serves 4.

∞

## Gebna Makleyah
## (Oven-Fried Cheese)

### Ingredients

1 cup firm feta cheese, crumbled, or traditional Egyptian cheese such as labna or gebna

1 Tablespoon flour

1 egg

Salt and freshly ground black pepper, to taste

Olive oil

Lemon wedges and pita bread cut into triangles, for serving

EPD Photos

*The dressing for Lemon and Garlic Potato Salad is a light and flavorful combination of lemon juice, garlic, and parsley.*

*With very clean hands, shape the Gebna Makleyah cheese mixture into balls about one inch in diameter.*

### Procedure

1. Preheat oven to 400°F.

2. Place the cheese, flour, egg, salt, and pepper in a bowl and mix well with very clean hands.

3. Roll the mixture into 1-inch balls.

4. If the mixture seems too loose to hold the ball shape, add a little more flour.

5. If the mixture seems too dry, add a bit of lemon juice, vinegar, or water.

6. Pour 2 or 3 Tablespoons olive oil onto a cookie sheet to grease.

7. Arrange the cheese balls on the cookie sheet, rolling them around to coat thoroughly with the oil.

8. Bake 5 minutes.

9. Wearing an oven mitt, open the oven door and shake the cookie sheet to prevent cheese balls from sticking and to turn them.

10. Bake 5 more minutes, until golden brown.

11. Remove with a spatula and drain on absorbent paper.

12. Serve warm with lemon wedges and triangles of pita bread.

Serves 4 to 6.

## 4 FOOD FOR RELIGIOUS AND HOLIDAY CELEBRATIONS

Approximately 90 percent of Egyptians are Muslims, which means they practice the religion of Islam. The most important time of the year for Muslims is a monthlong holiday called Ramadan. During the month of Ramadan (the ninth month on the Islamic calendar, usually November or December), Muslims fast (do not eat or drink) from sunrise to sunset, and think about people around the world who do not have enough food. Muslim families will often come together to prepare hearty meals, including a variety of sweets, after sunset. Muslims end Ramadan with a three-day celebration called *Eid al-Fitr.*

*Eid al-Adha,* a three-day long "great feast," is another important holiday for Muslims. In recognition of the Bible story of Abraham's sacrifice of his son, Jacob, families will sacrifice (kill) a sheep or a lamb. The animal is slaughtered and cooked whole on a spit over an open fire, and some of the meat is usually given to poorer families. These animals are also sacrificed on other important occasions, such as births, deaths, or marriages.

*A bakery displays loaves of bread on racks.*

Throughout the year, several *moulids* may take place. A moulid is a day (or as long as a week) celebrating the birthday of a local saint or holy person. Several events take place during this time. Food stands decorating the town's streets are usually set up near the holy person's tomb. Cairo, the capital of Egypt, celebrates at least three moulids every year. The largest moulid, Moulid el Nabit, commemorates the birthday of Muhammad and takes place in Cairo in early August.

Just under 10 percent of Egypt's population are Christians, whose most important holiday is Easter, falling in either March or April. It is common for families to come together to share a hearty meal, much as Christians worldwide do. Egyptian Christians observe the Orthodox calendar, which places Christmas on January 7 each year.

∞

## Bamia (Sweet and Sour Okra)

**Ingredients**

1 pound small okra pods

2 Tablespoons olive oil

1 Tablespoon honey

Salt and freshly ground black pepper, to taste

1 Tablespoon lemon juice, freshly squeezed

½ cup water

**Procedure**

1. Wash the okra and pat it dry with paper towels.

2. Discard any blemished or hard pods.

3. Heat the olive oil in a heavy saucepan and sauté the okra in the oil for 3 to 5 minutes, turning each pod once.

4. Add the honey, salt, pepper, lemon juice, and water. Cover, lower the heat, and simmer for 15 minutes, adding more water if necessary.

5. Serve hot.

Serves 4 to 6.

## 'Irea (Cinnamon Beverage)

**Ingredients**

2 cinnamon sticks

2 teaspoons sugar, or to taste

1 cup cold water

Mixed nuts

**Procedure**

1. Place the cinnamon and sugar in a small saucepan with the cold water and bring to a boil, stirring occasionally.

2. Lower the heat and allow the mixture to simmer for 10 minutes, or until it is brownish.

3. Remove the cinnamon sticks and pour the drink into a cup.

4. Serve with mixed nuts sprinkled into the cup.

Makes 1 cup.

## Khoshaf

**Ingredients**

1 cup dried prunes

1 cup dried apricots

1 cup dried small figs, halved

1½ cups raisins

1 cup sugar, or to taste

2½ cups boiling water

**Procedure**

1. Place all the fruits in a bowl and mix together gently.

2. Sprinkle the sugar on top of the dried fruits.

3. Carefully pour the boiling water into the bowl, cover, and allow to cool to room temperature.

4. Refrigerate for several hours, or overnight if possible. (*Khoshaf* is best when allowed to marinate overnight or for several hours before serving.)

Serves 4.

## Lettuce Salad

**Ingredients**

1 small head of lettuce, shredded

¾ cup orange juice

Pinch of salt

1½ teaspoons pepper, or to taste

**Procedure**

1. Toss lettuce with orange juice.

2. Season with a pinch of salt and pepper.

Makes 6 to 8 servings.

## 5 MEALTIME CUSTOMS

Dining customs vary throughout the country and between different religions. When guests are in the presence of Muslims (who make up approximately 90 percent of Egypt's population), there are some general guidelines one should follow. The left hand is considered unclean and should not be used for eating, feet should always been tucked under the table, and alcohol and pork should not be requested.

When invited to be a guest in an Egyptian household, it is polite for guests to bring a small gift to the host, such as flowers or chocolate, to show their appreciation for the meal. Before dinner, cocktails (often nonalcoholic) are frequently served. This is a time for socializing and becoming acquainted. *Mezze* (salads and dips) would also be served at this time. When dinner is ready, usually between 9 P.M. and 10 P.M., guests seat themselves and food is placed in the middle of the table. Bread will almost always accompany meals, which may include vegetables, rice dishes, soups, and meat dishes. Following dinner, guests will move into another room and enjoy coffee or mint tea. Guests should always compliment the cook.

Most Egyptian peasants cannot afford a large meal. Their diet includes vegetables, lentils, and beans. Meat, which is more costly, is eaten on special occasions. Most middle-class families eat a similar diet, but add more expensive ingredients when they can afford to. All social classes, however, enjoy quick bites at Egyptian cafes or street vendors. Traditional teahouses will serve tea in tall glasses (rather than teacups) and cafes normally offer strong, sweet Turkish coffee. Street vendors sell a variety of inexpensive foods, including *ful* (fava beans) and *koushari* (a macaroni, rice, and lentil dish) as a lunchtime favorite. Vendors also sell a variety of *asiir* (fresh-squeezed juices) made from fruits like banana, guava, mango, pomegranate, strawberry, from sugar cane, and even hibiscus flowers.

## Spinach with Garlic

### Ingredients

1 medium onion, chopped

1 Tablespoon vegetable oil

2 garlic cloves, chopped

1 can (15-ounce) tomato sauce

10 ounces frozen spinach, thawed

½ cup water

2 cups cooked rice

### Procedure

1. Heat oil in a large skillet.

2. Add onions and cook, stirring with a wooden spoon, until onions are softened.

3. Add the garlic and continue to cook for 2 minutes.

4. Add the tomato sauce and bring to a boil.

5. Simmer for 10 minutes on low heat.

6. Add the spinach and water, and heat to a boil again.

7. Cover and simmer on low heat for 15 minutes.

8. Serve warm over cooked rice.

Serves 4.

EPD Photos/Sana Abed-Kotob

*In Cairo, Egypt, a young vendor pushes sugarcane stalks through a commercial juice extractor. Behind him is a supply of sugarcane, cultivated on the farms of Upper (southern) Egypt.*

## 6 POLITICS, ECONOMICS, AND NUTRITION

In 1999, agriculture made up approximately 16 percent of Egypt's economy, employing about one-third of all Egyptians. However, Egypt's agriculture is also contributing to the slowing of economic growth. A shortage of arable land (land that can be farmed) has become a serious problem. The lack of farmable land has caused Egyptian farmers to move to other countries.

Irrigation necessary to grow its major crops, such as sugar cane, barley, wheat, corn, cotton, and rice, is also a growing problem. The Nile River is Egypt's main water source for both drinking and irrigation, and overuse could risk the country's delicate water supply. More than two thousand years ago, the Greek historian Herodotus wrote: "Egypt is the gift of the Nile." Without the Nile River, Egypt would be virtually dry and crops to prevent hunger and malnutrition could not grow. Much in part to the irrigation from the Nile River, Egypt has one of the lowest childhood malnourishment rates on the continent. About 9 percent of children younger than five were considered malnourished.

## 7 FURTHER STUDY

### Books

APA Productions. *Insight Guide: Egypt.* New York: Langenscheidt Publishers, 1999.

Balkwill, Richard. *Food and Feasts in Ancient Egypt.* New York: New Discovery, 1994.

Haag, Michael. *Cadogan Guide to Egypt.* London: Cadogan Books, 1998.

Hachten, Harva. *Best of Regional African Cooking.* New York: Hippocrene Books, Inc., 1998.

Imeme, Sally-Anne, and Stefan Cucos, eds. *Odyssey Guides: Egypt.* Chicago: Passport Books, 1997.

*Lonely Planet: Egypt.* 5th ed. Victoria, Australia: Lonely Planet Publications Pty Ltd., 1999.

Mallos, Tess. *The Complete Middle East Cookbook.* Boston: Tuttle, 1993.

### Web Sites

Recipes for Food and Cuisine in Egypt. [Online] Available http://touregypt.net/recipes/ (accessed January 28, 2001).

# Ethiopia

## Recipes

Kategna ................................................................. 144
Berbere (Spice Paste)........................................ 144
Niter Kebbeh or Kibe (Spiced Butter) ........................ 145
Injera (Ethiopian Bread)............................................ 146
Lab (Ethiopian Cheese) ............................................ 146
Kitfo (Spiced Raw Beef) ............................................ 147
Dabo Kolo (Little Fried Snacks)................................. 147
Aterkek Alecha (Vegetable Stew) .............................. 148

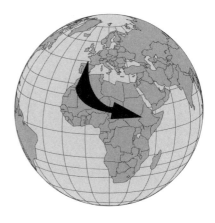

## 1 GEOGRAPHIC SETTING AND ENVIRONMENT

Situated in eastern Africa, Ethiopia (formerly called Abyssinia) has an area of approximately 1,127,127 square kilometers (435,186 square miles). Comparatively, the area occupied by Ethiopia is slightly less than twice the size of the state of Texas.

Ethiopia is a country of geographic contrasts, varying from as much as 125 meters (410 feet) below sea level in the Denakil depression to more than 4,600 meters (15,000 feet) above sea level in the mountainous regions. It contains a variety of distinct topographical zones: the Great Rift Valley runs the entire length of the country northeast-southwest; the Ethiopian Highlands are marked by mountain ranges; the Somali Plateau (Ogaden) covers the entire southeastern section of the country; and the Denakil Desert reaches to the Red Sea and the coastal foothills of Eritrea. Ethiopia's largest lake, Lake T'ana, is the source of the Blue Nile River.

The central plateau has a moderate climate with minimal seasonal temperature variation. The mean minimum during the coldest season is 6°C (43°F), while the mean maximum rarely exceeds 26°C (79°F). Temperature variations in the lowlands are much greater, and the heat in the desert and Red Sea coastal areas is extreme, with occasional highs of 60°C (140°F).

## 2 HISTORY AND FOOD

Ethiopia was under Italian military control for a period (1935–46) when Benito Mussolini (1883–1945) was in power. Except for that time, Ethiopian culture has been influenced very little by other countries. Ethiopia's mountainous terrain prevented its neighbors from exercising much influence over the country and its customs. Exotic spices were introduced to Ethiopian cooking by traders traveling the trade routes between Europe and the Far East.

Ethiopia went through a period of recurring drought and civil war during 1974–91. In 1991 a new government took over, and civil tensions were relieved somewhat because the coastal territory seceded from the inland government, creating the new nation of Eritrea.

Ethiopian cooking is very spicy. In addition to flavoring the food, the spices also help to preserve meat in a country where refrigeration is rare.

*Berbere* (pronounced bare-BARE-ee) is the name of the special spicy paste that Ethiopians use to preserve and flavor foods. According to Ethiopian culture, the woman with the best berbere has the best chance to win a good husband.

∞

## *Kategna*

### Ingredients

Large flat bread (flour tortilla, lavosh, or other "wrap" bread)

3 Tablespoons Cajun spices

2 teaspoons garlic powder

½ stick (4 Tablespoons) unsalted butter, softened

### Procedure

1. Preheat oven to 250°F.
2. Mix the garlic powder, spices, and butter together to make a spread.
3. Spread a thin layer over a piece of flat bread.
4. Place the bread on a cookie sheet, and bake for about 20 minutes, until crispy.

∞

## *Berbere*
## *(Spice Paste)*

### Ingredients

1 teaspoon ground ginger

½ teaspoon ground cardamom

½ teaspoon ground coriander

½ teaspoon fenugreek seeds

¼ teaspoon ground nutmeg

⅛ teaspoon ground cloves

⅛ teaspoon ground cinnamon

⅛ teaspoon ground allspice

2 Tablespoons onion, finely chopped

1 Tablespoon garlic, finely chopped

2 Tablespoons salt

3 Tablespoons red wine vinegar

2 cups paprika

1 to 2 Tablespoons red pepper flakes (use larger quantity to make a hotter paste)

½ teaspoon black pepper

1½ cups water

2 Tablespoons vegetable oil

**Procedure**

1. Measure the ginger, cardamom, coriander, fenugreek seeds, nutmeg, cloves, cinnamon, and allspice into a large frying pan.

2. Toast the spices over medium-high heat for 1 minute, shaking the pan or stirring with a wooden spoon constantly.

3. Let cool for 10 minutes.

4. Put the spices, onions, garlic, salt, and vinegar in a blender and mix at high speed until the spices form a paste.

5. Toast the paprika, red pepper flakes, and black pepper in the large frying pan for 1 minute, stirring constantly.

6. Add the water slowly to the pan, then add the vegetable oil.

7. Put the blender mixture into the pan as well, and cook everything together for 15 minutes stirring constantly.

8. Place the paste in a jar and refrigerate.

Makes 2 cups.

∞

## Niter Kebbeh or Kibe (Spiced Butter)

**Ingredients**

4 teaspoons fresh ginger, finely grated

1½ teaspoons tumeric

¼ teaspoon cardamom seeds

1 cinnamon stick, 1-inch long

⅛ teaspoon nutmeg

3 whole cloves

2 pounds salted butter

1 small yellow onion, peeled and coarsely chopped

3 Tablespoons garlic, peeled and finely chopped

**Ingredients**

1. Melt the butter in a heavy saucepan over moderate heat.

2. Bring the butter up to a light boil.

3. When the surface is covered with a white foam, stir in the remaining ingredients, including the onion and garlic.

4. Reduce the heat to low and cook uncovered for about 45 minutes. Do not stir again. Milk solids will form in the bottom of the pan and they should cook until they are golden brown. The butter will be clear.

5. Strain the mixture through several layers of cheesecloth placed in a strainer.

6. Discard the milk solids left in the cheesecloth.

7. Serve on toast, crackers, or use in cooking.

8. Store the spiced butter in a jar, covered, in the refrigerator (where it can keep up to 3 months).

## 3 FOODS OF THE ETHIOPIANS

The national dish of Ethiopia is *wot*, a spicy stew. *Wot* may be made from beef, lamb, chicken, goat, or even lentils or chickpeas, but it always contains spicy *berbere*. *Alecha* is a less-spicy stew seasoned with green ginger. For most Ethiopians, who are either Orthodox Christian or Muslim, eating pork is forbidden. Ethiopian food is eaten with the hands, using pieces of a type of flat bread called *injera*. Diners tear off a piece of *injera*, and then use it to scoop up or pinch off mouthfuls of food from a large shared platter. A soft white cheese called *lab* is popular. Although Ethiopians rarely use sugar in their cooking, honey is occasionally used as a sweetener. An Ethiopian treat is *injera* wrapped around a slab of fresh honeycomb with young honeybee grubs still inside. *Injera* is usually made from *teff,* a kind of grain grown in Ethiopia. The bread dough is fermented for several days in a process similar to that used to make sourdough bread. Usually enough bread is made at one time for three days. Little fried snacks called *dabo kolo* are also popular.

## Injera (Ethiopian Bread)

### Ingredients

1 cup buckwheat pancake mix

¾ cup all-purpose flour

3 teaspoons baking powder

1 cup club soda

½ teaspoon salt

1 beaten egg

2 Tablespoons butter

### Procedure

1. Mix buckwheat pancake mix, all-purpose flour, salt, and baking powder together in a medium bowl.

2. Add egg and club soda, and stir with a wooden spoon to combine.

3. Melt about 1 Tablespoon of the butter in a skillet until bubbly.

4. Pour in about 2 Tablespoons of batter and cook for 2 minutes on each side until the bread is golden brown on both sides.

5. Remove the bread from the pan carefully to a plate.

6. Repeat, stacking the finished loaves on the plate to cool.

EPD Photos

*The lab mixture, held in a cheesecloth sack and hung from the faucet, should drain for several hours.*

## Lab (Ethiopian Cheese)

### Ingredients

16 ounces (1 pound) cottage cheese

4 Tablespoons plain yogurt

1 Tablespoon lemon rind, grated

2 Tablespoons parsley, chopped

1 teaspoon salt

¼ teaspoon black pepper

### Procedure

1. Combine all the ingredients in a bowl.
2. Place a clean piece of cheesecloth (or a very clean dishtowel) in a colander and pour mixture into the colander to drain off extra liquid.
3. Gather the cheesecloth to make a sack and tie it with clean string or thread.
4. Suspend from the faucet over the sink. (Another option is to suspend the sack over a bowl by tying the string to the knob of a cupboard door.)
5. Allow to drain for several hours until the mixture has the consistency of soft cream cheese.
6. Serve with crackers or injera.

## Kitfo (Spiced Raw Beef)

### Ingredients

⅛ cup niter kebbeh (spiced butter, see recipe above)

¼ cup onions, finely chopped

2 Tablespoons green pepper, finely chopped

1 Tablespoon chili powder

½ teaspoon ginger, ground

¼ teaspoon garlic, finely chopped

¼ teaspoon cardamom, ground

½ Tablespoon lemon juice

1 teaspoon *berbere* (see recipe above)

1 teaspoon salt

1 pound ground beef

### Procedure

1. Melt the niter kebbeh in a large frying pan.
2. Add onions, green pepper, chili powder, ginger, garlic, and cardamom, and cook for 2 minutes while stirring.
3. Let cool for 15 minutes.

4. Add lemon juice, *berbere*, and salt.
5. Stir in raw beef and serve.

Serves 6.

## Dabo Kolo (Little Fried Snacks)

### Ingredients

2 cups all-purpose flour

½ teaspoon salt

2 Tablespoons honey

½ teaspoon cayenne pepper

¼ cup oil

### Procedure

1. Mix all the ingredients together in a bowl.
2. Add water slowly to create a stiff dough.
3. Knead on a lightly floured board for about 5 minutes. (To knead, flatten the dough, fold in half. Then turn the dough about one-quarter turn, and fold again. Keep turning and folding the dough.)
4. Pull off pieces of dough to fit on the palm of the hand.
5. Press or roll out (using a rolling pin) into a strip about ½-inch thick on a floured countertop.
6. Cut the strip into squares ½-inch by ½-inch.
7. Cook in a frying pan on medium heat until light brown in color on all sides.

## 4 FOOD FOR RELIGIOUS AND HOLIDAY CELEBRATIONS

About half of the Ethiopian population is Orthodox Christian. During Lent, the forty days preceding the Christian holiday of Easter, Orthodox Christians are prohibited from eating any animal products (no meat,

eaten. This sausage is made with beef, onions, pepper, ginger, cumin, basil, cardamom, cinnamon, cloves, and tumeric. It is smoked and dried.

∽

### Aterkek Alecha (Vegetable Stew)

**Ingredients**

1 cup vegetable oil (used as ¼ cup and ¾ cup)

2 cups red onion, chopped

2 cups yellow split peas

1 teaspoon salt

½ teaspoon ground ginger

⅛ teaspoon turmeric

3 cups water

**Procedure**

1. Pour ¼ cup oil into a large pot and place over medium heat.
2. Add onion and cook, stirring often, until the onion is golden brown.
3. Add ¾ cup oil and add all other ingredients.
4. Cook over medium heat until the vegetables are tender.
5. Serve with *injera* made with vegetable oil instead of butter.

### 5 MEALTIME CUSTOMS

Before eating a meal Ethiopians wash their hands under water poured from a pitcher into a basin. Then a prayer or grace is said. An appetizer of a bowl of curds and whey may be served. At the start of the meal, *injera* is layered directly on a round, woven basket table called a *mesob*. Different kinds of stews such as *wot* (spicy) and *alecha* (mild) are arranged on top of the *injera*.

---

> ### Some food words from Ethiopia:
>
> *berbere*. A paste, composed of hot spices, used to season many foods.
>
> *injera*. Spongy, fermented bread that tastes similar to sourdough bread and resembles a large flour torilla or large, thin pancakes
>
> *kitfo*. Raw beef dish.
>
> *teff*. A grain used to make teff flour, the basis for the national bread, injera
>
> *tib*. Generic name for cooked meat dishes
>
> *wot*. Spicy stews. If a dish has "wot" in its name, it will be hot, while "alecha" means mild.

cheese, milk, or butter). Instead they eat dishes made from beans, lentils, and chickpeas called *mitin shiro* that is a mixture of beans and *berbere*. This is made with lentils, peas, field peas, chick peas, and peanuts. The beans are boiled, roasted, ground, and combined with *berbere*. This mixture is made into a vegetarian *wot* by adding vegetable oil and then is shaped like a fish or an egg; it is eaten cold. A vegetable *alecha* may also be eaten during Lent.

During festive times such as marriage feasts, *kwalima*, a kind of beef sausage, is

Cory Langley

*An Ethiopian boy displays the produce, including peppers, squash, and grains, his family is offering for sale in the central market.*

Sometimes the meal will not begin until the head of the household or guest of honor tears off a piece of bread for each person at the table. The right hand is used to pick up a piece of *injera*, wrap some meat and vegetables inside, and eat. As a sign of respect, an Ethiopian may find the best piece of food on the table and put it in their guest's mouth. Ethiopians drink *tej* (a honey wine) and *tella* (beer) with their meals. Coffee, however, the most popular beverage in the country, is usually drunk at the end of a meal. Ethiopia is considered the birthplace of coffee. Coffee is a principal export.

The coffee, or *buna*, ceremony begins by throwing some freshly cut grasses in one corner of the room. Incense is lit in this corner next to a charcoal burner, where charcoal is glowing and ready to roast the coffee. All the guests watch while the raw green coffee beans are roasted. The host shakes the roasting pan to keep the beans from scorching and to release the wonderful aroma of the beans. The beans are then ground with a mortar and pestle (a bowl and pounding tool). A pot is filled with water, the fresh ground coffee is added, and the pot is placed on the charcoal burner until the water boils. The coffee is then served, often with a sprig of rue (a bitter-tasting herb with a small yellow flower). The same grounds may be used for two more rounds of coffee.

## 6 POLITICS, ECONOMICS, AND NUTRITION

Approximately half of the population of Ethiopia is classified as undernourished by the World Bank. This means they do not receive adequate nutrition in their diet. Of children under the age of five, about 48 percent are underweight, and nearly 64 percent are stunted (short for their age).

Wars, drought, political unrest, and population pressures of the 1970s and early 1980s have left their mark on the health of Ethiopians. Hundreds of thousands of people died during a famine (widespread food shortage) in 1973, and as many as one million may have died between 1983 and 1985. Ethiopia's coffee farmers produce one of the largest coffee crops in Africa; however, food crops are mainly produced by small farmers, known as subsistence farmers, who attempt to grow just enough food to feed their family. These farmers are not as successful. Ethiopians continues to suffer from malnutrition and a general lack of food. Sanitation (toilets and sewers to carry away human waste) is a problem as well, with only one-fifth of the population having access to adequate sanitation. Between 1994 and 1995, a little over one-quarter had access to safe drinking water.

## 7 FURTHER STUDY

### Books

Amin, Mohamed. *Spectrum Guide to Ethiopia.* New York: Interlink Publishing Group, Inc., 2000.

Harris, Jessica B. *The Africa Cookbook: Tastes of a Continent.* New York: Simon & Schuster, 1998.

Merson, Annette. *African Cookery.* Nashville, TN: Winston-Derek Publishers, Inc., 1987.

Sandler, Bea. *The African Cookbook.* New York: First Carol Publishing Group, 1983.

### Web Sites

Ethiopian Resources. [Online] Available http://www.ethiopianresources.com (accessed February 28, 2001).

IWon. [Online] Available http://advertise.iwon.com/home/food_n_drink/globaldest_overview/0,15463,250,00.html (accessed March 23, 2001).

Lonely Planet. [Online] Available http://www.lonelyplanet.com/destinations/africa/ethiopia/culture.htm (accessed March 23, 2001).

Spiced Butter Recipe. [Online] Available http://www.wube.net/butter.html (accessed June 13, 2001).

World Gourmet. [Online] Available http://www.globalgourmet.com/destinations/ethiopia/ethiback.html (accessed March 23, 2001).

# France

## Recipes

Baguette (French Bread)............................................ 152
Baguette Sandwich ................................................... 153
Soupe à l'Oignon Gratinée (Onion Soup)................. 153
Croque-Monsieur (Ham and Cheese Sandwich) ........ 154
Quiche au Saumon et Crevettes (Quiche)................. 155
Mousse au Chocolat (Chocolate Mousse)................. 155
Fromage (Cheese Board)........................................ 156
Bûche de Noël (Yule Log)....................................... 156
La Galette des Rois (King's Cake)............................ 157

## 1 GEOGRAPHIC SETTING AND ENVIRONMENT

France is the second-largest country in Europe (after Russia). Much of the country is surrounded by mountains. The highest mountain, Mount Blanc, is near France's border with Italy. The climate and soil of France create good conditions for farming. Although only four percent of the French people earn their living from farming, the country is self-sufficient when it comes to growing its own food.

## 2 HISTORY AND FOOD

The French have always been proud of their sophisticated way of cooking. Fertile soil provides fresh fruits, vegetables, herbs, grains, and meat, nearly year-round. The soil is also suitable for growing grapes, which are used for making some of the finest wines in the world. Food and alcohol play important roles in French society—the way a person eats often reflects their French heritage, region of birth, social status, and health.

During the reign of Louis XIV (1661–1715), the nobility (upper class citizens) would hold twelve-hour feasts with over ten different dishes served. The presentation of the food was just as important as the taste and quality of the ingredients. Such elaborate feasts were too expensive and required too much time for the common people to prepare for themselves, but others were also able to enjoy exotic foods and spices, such as the kumquat fruit and yellow saffron, brought back from Africa and Asia by explorers. These foods were quickly incorporated into the French diet.

## 3 FOODS OF THE FRENCH

The baguette, a long, thin loaf of crusty bread, is the most important part of any French meal. Everyone at the table is expected to eat a piece. It is eaten in a variety of ways, including being used to make

Lotte fish that can only be found in the Loire River. On the coasts of France seafood is plentiful, including mussels, clams, oysters, shrimp, and squid. The French enjoy *escargots* (snails) cooked with garlic and butter, roast duck, and rabbit.

∞

## Baguette (French Bread)

### Ingredients

1 package dry yeast

1 Tablespoon salt

2 Tablespoons sugar

2½ cups warm water

7 cups flour

Egg white, lightly beaten

### Procedure

1. Grease two cookie sheets.

2. Dissolve the yeast, salt, and sugar in water in a large mixing bowl.

3. Stir in the flour until a stiff dough forms. Turn the dough onto a floured surface (countertop or cutting board) and knead for 10 minutes.

4. Clean out the mixing bowl, lightly oil it, and return the dough to the bowl.

5. Cover the bowl with plastic wrap. Let the dough rise until doubled in size, ½ hour or so.

6. Dip your fist in flour and push your fist into the center of the dough to "punch" it down. Remove from the bowl, and knead 3 or 4 more times.

7. Separate the dough into 4 equal pieces. Form each piece into a long loaf. Place 2 on each of the greased cookie sheets.

8. Carefully slash the top diagonally every few inches with a knife.

sandwiches. Melted cheese spread on a baguette is often presented as part of a meal. A meal of grilled food (called *la raclette*) is sometimes served. Using an open grill, diners melt their own cheese with ham or beef slices, or fry their own egg. The grilled food is accompanied by potatoes. Sometimes diners spear pieces of bread on long-handled forks, and dip the bread into a pot full of melted cheese called *la fondue*.

The regions of France have varying cuisine: in Brittany (northwestern France), the main dish is *crêpes* (thin pancakes) with cider; and in the Alsace region (eastern France near Germany), a popular dish is cabbage with pieces of sausage, called *la choucroute*. The French from the Loire River Valley eat a special dish made of the

9. Brush the loaves with the egg white. Cover lightly with plastic wrap and let the loaves rise again for about 30 minutes.

10. Preheat oven to 400°F. Bake loaves for 10 minutes.

11. Lower heat to 350°F and bake 20 more minutes.

## Baguette Sandwich

### Ingredients

1 small baguette (purchased or freshly baked; see recipe above)

Cheese (may be soft cheese, such as Brie, or hard cheese, such as Gouda)

Ham

Tomato

Leaf lettuce

Mayonnaise or mustard

Cornichons (tiny sweet French pickles)

### Procedure

1. Slice the baguette in half lengthwise.

2. Spread one half with mayonnaise or mustard, depending on preference.

3. Arrange sliced cheese and ham over the mayonnaise.

4. Slice the sweet pickles in half, and arrange on ham.

5. Top with sliced tomato and lettuce.

6. Wrap in plastic wrap and carry for lunch away from home.

Serves 1 or 2.

EPD Photos

*A uniquely French accent to the filling of the Baguette Sandwich are the cornichons (French pickles).*

## Soupe à l'Oignon Gratinée (Onion Soup)

### Ingredients

½ pound onions, cut into thin slices

3 ounces Swiss cheese, grated

1 Tablespoon butter

3 Tablespoons olive oil

1 cup white wine (optional) or water

1 Tablespoon flour

1 beef bouillon cube and a dash of Worcestershire sauce (optional)

3 cups water

Four ¾-inch thick slices of bread, cut from a baguette

Salt and pepper

### Procedure

1. Melt the butter and olive oil in large saucepan over medium heat and add the onions.
2. Brown the onions for about 5 minutes.
3. Sprinkle the flour on onions and stir until dissolved, heating 5 more minutes.
4. Add the wine (if desired) and the water.
5. Add salt and pepper to taste.
6. Add the bouillon cube and dash of Worcestershire sauce (if desired).
7. Simmer for 20 minutes.
8. Pour soup into bowls. Float a slice of bread in each bowl.
9. Top the hot soup with cheese.

Serves 4.

∞

### Croque-Monsieur (Ham and Cheese Sandwich)

#### Ingredients

1 loaf (12 slices) of sandwich bread

8 slices of ham

8 slices of Swiss cheese

Swiss cheese, grated

1 cup milk

1 Tablespoon butter

2 Tablespoons flour

Salt and pepper

#### Procedure

1. Preheat oven to 400°F.
2. Place a slice of ham and a slice of cheese between two pieces of bread; repeat this step on the same sandwich to make a triple-decker sandwich.
3. Repeat to make 4 sandwiches in all. Arrange the sandwiches in a baking dish.

EPD Photos

*These triple-decker croque-monsieurs (ham and cheese sandwiches) will be covered with a creamy sauce and topped with shredded Swiss cheese before baking.*

4. *Make the béchamel:* Combine the flour, milk, butter, salt, and pepper in a saucepan. Heat over low heat, stirring constantly with a wire whisk, until the flour has completely dissolved.
5. Pour the *béchamel* (white sauce) mixture over the sandwiches and top with the grated Swiss cheese.
6. Bake for 15 minutes, or until the cheese is melted and crusty.
7. Serve on 4 plates. Cut sandwiches into halves or quarters.

Serves 4.

## Quiche au Saumon et Crevettes (Salmon and Shrimp Quiche)

### Ingredients

1 prepared pie crust

4 small pieces of smoked salmon

1 small can of little shrimp

Swiss cheese, grated

½ cup sour cream

3 eggs

Salt and pepper

### Procedure

1. Preheat oven to 350°F.
2. Beat the eggs until light and fluffy.
3. Add the sour cream and cheese to the eggs and beat again.
4. Poke holes in the bottom of the pie crust with a fork.
5. Cover the bottom of the crust with the salmon. Arrange the shrimp evenly on top of salmon.
6. Pour the egg mixture over the seafood. Bake for 25 minutes.
7. Cut pie into quarters and serve hot with a salad and crusty bread.

Serves 4.

## Mousse au Chocolat (Chocolate Mousse)

*Packaged instant chocolate mousse mix, simpler to prepare than this traditional recipe, is available at most grocery stores and may be substituted.*

### Ingredients

4 ounces unsweetened cooking chocolate

4 eggs, separated

½ cup sugar

1 cup heavy cream

Pinch of salt

Raspberries, strawberries, and ladyfinger cookies as accompaniment

### Procedure

1. Melt the chocolate over low heat in a saucepan.
2. Remove from heat, add cream and allow mixture to cool.
3. Separate egg whites from the yolks.
4. Add sugar to the yolks and mix well.
5. Add yolk mixture to chocolate in the saucepan.
6. Add a pinch of salt to egg whites, then beat with an electric mixer until stiff.
7. Stir egg whites gently into chocolate mixture and let cool in the refrigerator for at least 4 hours.
8. To serve, arrange ladyfinger cookies vertically around the mousse.
9. Arrange fresh fruit such as strawberries or raspberries on top. Serve chilled.

Serves 2 to 4.

## 4 FOOD FOR RELIGIOUS AND HOLIDAY CELEBRATIONS

Major French holidays include Christmas (December 25), New Year's Day (January 1), and Bastille Day (July 14). On Bastille Day, named for the prison that citizens stormed on July 14, 1789, the French celebrate their liberation (freedom) from the monarchy and the beginning of their Republic. There are fireworks, dances, and parties with picnics. Picnics almost always include fromage (cheese), such as Camembert, brie, chevre (goat's milk cheese), or Roquefort.

∞

## Fromage
### (Cheese Board)

### Ingredients

¼ to ½ pound of 3 different cheeses: select from Camembert, brie, chevre (goat's milk), Roquefort (bleu cheese)

1 loaf of crusty French bread (or 1 package of crackers)

Wooden cutting board for cheese

Basket for bread or crackers

Cheese knife or paring knife

### Procedure

1. Arrange the cheeses on the wooden cutting board.

2. Line the basket with a napkin (*serviette* in French), and fill it with crackers or the bread, sliced into thin rounds.

3. Diners will use the knife to cut their own individual slices of cheese. Serve at room temperature.

Serves 12 or more.

For Christmas, the French have large feasts with many courses, which usually end with a *Bûche de Noël,* or Yule log. This cake is shaped to look like a log of wood because of the traditional French custom of lighting a real log at Christmas. On the first Sunday of January, the Christian holiday, Epiphany, is celebrated, marking the three kings' visit to the newborn baby Jesus. For this occasion, a special dessert called *la galette des rois,* is prepared. A small token, either a bean or porcelain toy, is baked inside. Whoever finds the hidden bean or porcelain toy in their piece gets to be king or queen for the day and wear a golden crown. Traditionally, the king (the man who found the bean in his piece of cake) had to pick a queen and present her with a gift. To avoid this obligation, the "king" would sometimes eat the evidence. To solve this problem, in 1874 French bakers began putting collectible porcelain charms in their cakes instead of beans.

∞

## Bûche de Noël (Yule Log)

4 eggs

1 cup sugar

3 Tablespoons water

1 cup cake flour

1½ teaspoons cornstarch

1½ teaspoons baking powder

¼ teaspoon salt

½ teaspoon almond extract

½ teaspoon vanilla

Large jar of seedless jelly (strawberry or raspberry)

Chocolate frosting, 1 can

Powdered sugar

Optional decorations: holly berries and evergreen leaves (fresh or artificial)

### Procedure

1. Preheat oven to 400°F.

2. Grease a jelly-roll pan (cookie sheet with a rim all around) and line the bottom with waxed paper. Grease the waxed paper well.

3. Beat the eggs until frothy and pale yellow in a large mixing bowl.

4. Add the sugar and water to the eggs and continue to beat.

5. Mix flour, cornstarch, baking powder, and salt in a separate bowl.

6. Add the flour mixture to egg mixture.

7. Add the vanilla and almond extract.

8. Pour the batter into the prepared pan.

9. Bake for 15 minutes. (Toothpick inserted into the center should come out clean. Do not overbake.)

10. Remove from oven. Cover pan with a clean dishtowel, and turn over to remove cake from pan. Remove pan and carefully peel off the wax paper. (Cake is wrong-side up.) Trim off any crusty edges.

11. Fold one end of towel over short end of cake, and carefully roll cake up inside the towel.

12. Lift the whole roll and place it, seam side down on a cooling rack.

13. Allow to cool completely. Unroll carefully.

14. Coat the cake completely with jelly.

15. Carefully roll the cake back up again, without the towel.

16. Cut a 2-inch slice from one end and cut in half.

17. Attach these pieces to the sides of the cake to resemble branch stubs on a log.

18. Frost the cake "log" with chocolate icing. Drag a fork along the length of the cake, scoring the frosting to resemble bark.

19. Arrange holly berries and evergreen leaves around the cake if desired.

Serves 12 or more.

∞

## La Galette des Rois (King's Cake)

1¼ pounds puff pastry (available in the frozen foods section of the supermarket)

1 dry bean (such as a dried kidney bean or navy bean)

2 eggs

7 ounces almond paste

Paper crown for decoration

**Procedure**

1. Preheat oven to 425°F.

2. Grease a cookie sheet.

3. Roll out pastry an 8-inch round.

4. Mix 1 egg with the almond paste until smooth and spread evenly onto the pastry.

5. Place the bean anywhere on the filling.

6. Roll out another 8-inch piece of pastry and place it over the almond filling. Press the edges together firmly to seal. Score the top layer lightly with a sharp knife.

7. Beat the other egg lightly and gently brush over the top layer.

8. Bake for 20 minutes. Lower the heat to 400°F, and bake for another 25 minutes.

9. Serve warm, with the crown on top.

Serves 8. The person who finds the bean is designated as the queen or king.

## 5 MEALTIME CUSTOMS

When entertaining at home, the hosts pride themselves on making mealtime a memorable and positive experience. For everyday lunches and dinners, four courses are typically served: salad, main dish with meat, cheese with bread, and dessert. Bread and water are always served. Special occasions include even more courses such as an appetizer of savory pastries, or other finger foods. This is normally served with an alcoholic beverage, often French wine. Several bottles of wine may be served with the meal. Coffee is also served.

Restaurants in France are generally more formal than those in the United States. It is expected that patrons are there to have a full meal. Wine is ordered by the half or full carafe (a glass container). Waiters are rarely tipped because a fee for service is added to the bill for the meal. Eating out is a social occasion, and is a leisurely activity. It is considered rude to ask to have leftover food wrapped to be taken home. Several fast food restaurants such as Quick (a French version of McDonald's), and Pizza Hut are available. Sidewalk vendors and cafés or local *boulangeries* (bakeries) also offer quick.

The typical eating habits of the French include three meals a day, with tea served at 4 P.M. Breakfast often includes a fresh baguette and buttery croissants, sometimes filled with chocolate or almond paste. Coffee, café, is usually very strong; café au lait is coffee served with hot milk. Fresh fruit and yogurt are also common at breakfast. Lunch is the main meal of the day and takes more time to eat than the typical lunch in the United States. For this reason, many businesses are closed between 12 noon and 2 P.M. A school lunch might consist of a baguette filled with cheese, butter, meat, lettuce, and tomato. Dinner usually takes place after eight at night.

## 6 POLITICS, ECONOMICS, AND NUTRITION

The diet of the French people is generally considered healthy, and most citizens receive adequate nutrition. In 2001 the countries of Europe experienced outbreaks of two diseases, "mad cow disease" and "hoof and mouth disease" that affected the cattle and sheep herds. Many countries enacted laws and regulations restricting the import and export of meat during that period, until the diseases could be brought under control. In France, there have been protests at some fast food restaurants in an attempt to drive them out of the country to keep the traditional quality of French food and the French lifestyle.

## 7 FURTHER STUDY

### Books

Denny, Roz. *A Taste of France.* New York: Thompson Learning, 1994.

Fisher, Teresa. *France.* Austin: Raintree Steck-Vaughn, 1999.

Langer, William L. *An Encyclopedia of World History.* 5th ed. Boston: Houghton Mifflin, 1980.

Loewen, Nancey. *Food in France.* Vero Beach: Rourke Publications, 1991.

### Web Sites

French Food and Cook. [Online] Available http://www.ffcook.com (accessed July 24, 2001).

French Information Center. [Online] Available http://www.france.com (accessed July 24, 2001).

Recipe Source. [Online] Available http://www.recipesource.com/ethnic/europe/french/ (accessed July 24, 2001).

### Films

*Babette's Feast.* Rated G. (1987)
This film is set in France in the late 1800s. During an uprising, a French chef named Babette is exiled to Denmark where she becomes maid and cook for two sisters. Babette spends years making simple meals for the sisters until one day she wins the French lottery. Babette uses her winnings to prepare an extravagant seven-course French meal for the sisters and ten other community members. The film depicts the lavish feast in detail, including the food preparation and consumption.